Cub Reporter

The Accrington Observer

By Irvine Hunt

Irvine Hunt is the author of nine books including the evocative *Road to Paradise* and *Norman Nicholson's Lakeland,* a prose anthology. A colourful literary life has included five years as a sub-editor for *The Daily Telegraph,* making a documentary film in Norway (after he had previously been deported), and spending seven months walking round Spain and Portugal.

He lives with his family in Cumbria.

Cub Reporter

The Accrington Observer

By the same author

The Drover's Boy, a novel, Handstand Press

Road to Paradise, short stories, CN Group

Lakeland Yesterday, period pictures,

Vol l, Smith-Settle; Vol 11, Waltersgill

Manlaff and Toewoman, poems, Rusland Press

Norman Nicholson's Lakeland,

a prose anthology, Robert Hale

On Kindle; *Dating the Witch*, short stories,
http://amzn.to/TyiXnc

Other e-book stories are pending.

For an excellent history about the cotton industry see
The Story of Lancashire Cotton by Ron Freethy

Published by Irvine Hunt.

www.irvinehunt.co.uk

Copyright © Irvine Hunt 2013

For Harry Birtwistle, Garth Dawson and
Audrey Eyton... who all had a part.

Illustrations by Judy Evans

My warm thanks to writer Josie Baxter who greatly encouraged the whole idea, to John Simpson, Local History Librarian, Accrington Library, who kept producing articles and copies of the *Observer* from the library's deepest depths, and to Maisie.

Contents

1. Job Hunt

ALL the days of study were over. It was June and sunlit again after a dull wet spring. I was twenty and it was time to find a job. Thanks to the help of a friend I had found temporary summer work on Fleetwood Pier as a key man. This meant patrolling the pier and looking after penny slot machines, opening them up when they jammed and stopping visitors from pounding them to pieces. I was given a long necklace of keys, a hundred or more which hung round my neck on chains in a giant tangle. A tangle and a responsibility. Take care of these, I was warned, they are valuable. Don't trust everyone you meet. One of the attendants had been attacked and the keys dragged off him.

On my second day one of the other key men, Lofty Albert (he was certainly tall) showed how one could increase one's weekly pay. At times visitors fed pennies into the slots almost in a stream and a surprising number failed to notice they had pushed in half-a-crown by mistake, both coins being the same size. The key men replaced a half-crown with one of their own pennies and regarded it as legal robbery.

In the evenings I wrote off to newspapers applying for jobs. More than anything I wanted to be a reporter. After years of asthma I was beginning to feel stronger and now at twenty I began to sense that I had a chance. Sometimes jobs as journalists were advertised in the trade papers, but mostly I wrote at random and soon had a heap of rejection letters. It was a slow dispiriting process and as summer passed September drew near and my job on the pier would soon draw to an end.

To vary the work, I was made an attendant at the Guess Your Weight machine. It was a popular job among the pier hands. At 2d a try people stood on the scales and the attendant had to guess the person's weight to within a few pounds. They would be paid a £1 prize out of our own pockets if we guessed wrongly. My misgivings at possibly losing a lot of money soon went. No matter how big or small the customer, it was always possible to get away with it. The pier hands, all men, were allowed to clutch at the arms of the men and women before they stepped onto the scales to assess how solid they were. This was supposed to be the skilled part of the challenge and among the attendants it was a popular part of the proceedings. The notice pinned over the scales said that one had to guess to within six pounds of the person's weight. In fact that made it to within twelve pounds, six pounds on either side. None of the attendants ever lost a penny and there were plenty of laughs and lots of grasping of female arms.

Time was running out. The holiday crowds were diminishing. Rain had returned and the wet days and an empty pier created a feeling of desolation.

At a bread and cake shop outside the pier the baker was often helping behind the counter, serving hot barm cakes, round soft flat bread rolls. Often he had a little joke. His dough, he said, had real pound notes in it. His rock buns were full of genuine rock. As jokes they were not up to much but the man himself was likeable and kind. You could tell he was a baker. Gradually he learned about the difficulties of getting a job on a newspaper.

"See," he said one lunchtime. "I've been waiting for you. I've saved you this."

He held a newspaper and pointed to an advertisement. "They want a junior reporter. It's in a small mill town where I used to live."

The paper was called the *Accrington Observer*. My first thought was how old-fashioned it looked. Its front page was covered in a grey mass of advertisements. But my hopes were not raised. The advertisement, like most of the others I had seen, suggested it wanted a school-leaver, a sixteen or eighteen-year-old, someone they could train up, not someone who was twenty.

Apply by letter before the month end.

The baker waved a hand. "Go on, try for it," he urged.

"Thank you, I'll write this weekend."

"No, no," he said. "Phone them now. Show them you want the job."

"It says write..."

"Ignore that. Phone them. I'll find you the number."

But as I hadn't any money I promised I would ring later.

He guessed. "Use my phone." He pointed at the receiver. "Go on. You can pay me at the weekend."

He overruled my doubts. He thumbed through the paper and found the number. He ushered me round the counter. He said they would expect a reporter to be enterprising. He dialled the number for me; he put the phone in my hand. He was just what I needed.

Almost at once the voice of the editor came on the line and for the next six or seven minutes he listened while I told him how I longed to be a reporter and how I had been writing after jobs now for weeks without success, and in fact had seventeen refusals.

 The man sounded cautious. He began to end the conversation by saying: "Well, really we are looking for someone younger, but put all this in a letter and we'll let you know."

Everything I had said, in a letter. A pang of dismay struck me. I hoped I could remember it all.

He added he would reply "within a week." And almost as an afterthought he said: "Why are you only just thinking about journalism?"

I told him I had had asthma since about nine years old and only now was I feeling stronger.

"Asthma?" he said. "Have you now? Well as it happens so have I."

Somehow the thought was reassuring.

Until now I had scarcely heard of Accrington, and never heard of the *Accrington Observer*, but spurred on by the baker I wrote a letter, and then rewrote it a couple more times, and posted it feeling that it still was not well enough written, and then for seven days I hoped that there would be no answer. I did not want an answer. Nor was there. It was exactly what I had hoped. My baker friend had talked about being enterprising, well I would be. He was right. The pier gave me the day off and I took the train inland to Accrington. I would arrive without invitation and try to see the editor in person. My excuse was that I had not had a reply.

East Lancashire... the train rattled through a dismal landscape and everywhere it seemed were mill chimneys, factories, dark skies and lines of gardenless houses climbing up hillsides. The more the train drew into factory Lancashire the gloomier grew the sky. From the railway carriage it was possible to peer down into choked backyards, some with a slab of stone on the roof of what I took to be lime-washed outside privies. Here and there were flashes of a bright pool or pond, or a field still used for crops, or a once grand house with tall chimneys. But elsewhere great stretches formed a weary landscape, small towns backed by dismal hills. It was not encouraging.

The train drew into Accrington station. It was drizzling as I walked down a road into the centre of a small hill town, apprehensive about the next half hour. Supposing no one would see me and my journey proved to be a waste of time? Having come this far there was no turning back. I asked a man to direct me to the *Observer* office. He showed the way. It was down a cobbled street near a looming railway viaduct.

The office looked a bit like a small shop. At a varnished counter I asked to see the editor. A white haired woman asked doubtfully if I had an appointment. There was only one approach: I told her the truth. "We've spoken on the phone about a job, and I've written a letter, but really I'm gate-crashing." It was feeble but all I could think of.

The woman's face did not change. "Are you now? Then you had better wait here while I find out if he'll see you. I know he's very busy."

She retreated to a telephone and held a whispered conversation with another part of the building.

"Well you're lucky because Mr Watson will see you," she said. She crooked a finger to show that I should follow.

We were swallowed by a gloomy staircase and passage. We walked along bare boards into the heart of the building and halted on a landing outside a shabby brown door.

The editor stood up and shook hands. Tom Watson was a small man with glasses and a worn chalk-striped suit. He face was tired but not unfriendly. A long interview followed. He asked if I did shorthand, if I typed, if I enjoyed writing, had I had anything published, had I been to Accrington before? All the questions I had answered on the phone. I told him my shorthand was a bit unpractised and I could type and enjoyed writing and had scarcely heard about Accrington until a week ago, except that I knew now it was a mill town, and it looked a bit grim.

He laughed at that. "Well you're honest, lad, and that's a start."

Mr Watson called in the assistant editor, a younger man who asked more questions. He was called Harry Crossley. He did not say much and I had a feeling he was unsure about me. Several other people opened the door and hung inside to ask about "Page five," and finally a reporter in hat and raincoat interrupted to say that the men at Bullough's were talking about a strike and should he get the story now, or leave it until court was over?

The editor said get the strike story and put someone else on the court.

The interview was over. He told me that there could be no decision yet about a job because a number of other applicants had to be seen first.

"But we'll let you know in a week."

That same promise.

He smiled and we shook hands.

As I left the office and went up the cobbled street I wondered if a letter really would come in a week. Would I dare to visit the editor again? The thought went round and round. I felt I had not exactly succeeded. The editor had said there were others he was going to interview. There could easily be a dozen or more, all like me after the job. I prayed that no letter would come. Given the chance I would visit the town again, without invitation. What had I to lose? I liked the look of the office, I liked the editor. I liked it all. Please don't write!

Back at Fleetwood Pier work was suddenly tedious. I told my friend the baker all that had happened. "You stand a chance," he said encouragingly. "The fact they did not say no right away shows that."

But I knew they wanted someone younger. Then it would cost less to train up a new reporter.

Another agonising week passed and no letter came. Excited, I took the train inland once more. Excited, and determined. Had they already decided, or were they still interviewing others?

Mr Watson saw me.

"I know I've come again, unannounced," I told him as we shook hands, "but I really do want this job."

He eyed me steadily through his glasses. "You do, don't you ...well sit down, lad."

It was only a guess on my part, but I began to hope. It seemed they had not yet decided.

This time he was less busy and he talked away for a long time. How local journalism was a good way to learn how to become a reporter.

That it was ninety-nine per cent hard work and little glamour.

I tried to assure him that I understood. Glamour simply wasn't my kind of thinking.

We looked through the latest copy of the *Observer*. The assistant editor Harry Crossley came into the room and shook hands. Again he was watchful but a shade friendlier.

"Perhaps you'd better come and have a look at the reporters' room," said the editor eventually. He stubbed out another cigarette, took a drink from a pint mug of tea and led the way across the passage.

Behind the bare plank door was a small office. No reporters were in but on every side were files, desks, empty mugs, typewriters and overflowing wire wastepaper baskets. It was immensely untidy but at once exciting.

"Do you think you'd like to work here?" said Mr Watson surveying the room.

"I would," I said.

"Right lad," he said, "then the job's yours."

I was singing in the heart of me as I walked up the street to the station. Back at home I packed my belongings in a suitcase, gave notice at my lodgings and told my employer on the pier that I would be leaving, that I had got a job as a reporter.

But most of all, I thanked the baker. "Without your help I'd not have gone on trying much longer."

"I'm glad for you," he said simply. "You'll like Accrington. It's where I learned to bake."

A few days later I got off the train in the little mill town for a third time. It was Sunday and November already. The streets were gloomy with weak afternoon sunshine. An occasional mill chimney stuck up among the houses, and the few people around hurried and were not lingering. Somehow the shops seemed small and the smaller roads dismally wet and cobbled. The railway viaduct loomed on tall stone and brick arches, overlooking the town as it curved from one end to the other. Everything was depressing looking, industrial, yet I did not feel depressed. First I would stop for a few days in a small hotel while I found somewhere good to live. And I'd get a proper coat. The weather was growing colder.

Down in the street near the viaduct, little Edgar Street, I stood in front of the *Observer* office. Tomorrow I would be a reporter.

2. First Morning

Monday morning, five to nine, I arrived at the front entrance and went up the little staircase. The editor smiled and shook my hand.

The reporters' room was occupied by half a dozen people. Typewriters stopped being hammered as Mr Watson led me in with Harry Crossley and introduced the new reporter. Hellos and handshakes, grins and some appraising looks.

"Frank Kitchener, sports editor; Rowland Joynson, district reporter; Fred Billington, our Rishton and Oswaldtwistle man; Geraldine – it's not her real name."

Geraldine smiled over the top of her typewriter. "She writes *Ladies' Chain,* the woman's column; Vic Throup, sport and general; Allan Lambert, chief court reporter - perfect shorthand, eh, Allan?"

"I wouldn't say that," said Allan.

"Others are up at Haslingden," said the editor, dusting cigarette ash off his trousers. "You'll meet them in time. Now find yourself a desk and make yourself at home."

He went out of the room with Harry Crossley, known as Mr Harry, and the typing began again. The *Observer* came out twice weekly, on Tuesdays and Saturdays. This meant that Mondays and Fridays were press days and everyone in the room was racing to finish stories for tomorrow's Tuesday edition.

Several grins came my way but I was left standing, feeling embarrassed. With all the work going on no one had realised that there wasn't an empty desk, or a spare chair either. Was this some sort of initiative test? I hoped not.

To avoid attention I turned to a board covered in yellowing notices. *"Mr Bradshaw has complained again that his initials are W. B. not WC, with full points please,"* said one. *"A WC is a lavatory.*

"Wayzgoose May 10; venue Blackpool." (Whatever was a wayzgoose?)

The editor returned, holding a sheet of paper covered in scrawl. "Here you are, get this written up." He paused to look around. "Where are you sitting?"

When I explained there wasn't a desk available everyone stopped typing and began to apologise. Under the editor's guidance a pile of bound volumes of the *Observer* was carried out and loaded into a cupboard and a table emerged. Mr Watson glared round the room. "I've told the lot of you before, put the files back on the shelves when you've done with them!"

A chair was produced from another room and I found myself sitting next to a grubby window with a lanky geranium in a pot on one side and a crushed wire wastepaper basket on the other. The window needed cleaning but through it I could see the railway viaduct, looming vaguely. Somehow it was reassuring, solid, industrial, a kind of symbol, though I kept the thought to myself.

As if to make up for the awkward welcome, a concerned man with grey eyes and wearing a long raincoat and a grey felt hat mumbled he was Rowland Joynson, and we shook hands, and then, talking non-stop, his eyes looking slightly to one side as he spoke, he explained that no one had noticed about the desk because they were all trying to get their weekend copy finished, and on the windowsill was a spare typewriter but the letter *e* key kept sticking, but worked if you banged it, and if I wanted copy paper to write on there was a pile on the other end of the windowsill, and there was a place where I could make the tea, and a small wash place outside the door on the left to wash the cups and mugs, and I could use the yellow cracked mug unless I had brought one of my own, and it would be better tomorrow if I did because they were short of crockery and the market hall sold cheap ones.

I hauled the typewriter off the windowsill, a solid Underwood, and set it down on my own desk. The feeling was good but the relief was replaced by a niggling dread of whether I would be able to write the reports well enough to satisfy Harry Crossley who was not only the assistant editor, but also the sub-editor and much else.

I need not have felt concern. My first story as a real journalist was easy. Two paragraphs. A *Scouts` Social.*

Soon a collection of small news items began to land in the pick-up basket on Mr Harry's desk, to be turned into readable stories – a Women's Guild coffee morning, a wedding, a lost Siamese cat, Penny, "loves children", and a heap of forms covered in writing, all of them funerals.

"If news is scarce," Mr Harry instructed, "include all the mourners and all the floral tributes. The biog first, then the mourners and the floral tributes last. But make sure the mourners and the tributes are in separate pars, and don't make the pars too long. The pages start looking too heavy.

"If we're stuck for space on press days we can chop off the floral tributes, but we try to keep in the lot if we can. Every name sells a copy."

Everyone in the room appeared to be expert at potted biographies. Almost every other funeral seemed to be a person who had worked at Howard and Bullough, the town's giant factory:

Mr John Bainbridge, who died at his home in Oak Street, aged 59, was a machinist at Howard and Bullough for 26 years. Before that he was a plate fitter at Messrs Holland's, having started there in his teens. He leaves a widow and six children.

The mourners were...

The reporters' room grew busier. Afternoon came. More short items needing rewriting, a bicycle theft, a meeting of a Ladies' Bright Hour, the Local Divorce Decrees, and a church choir concert in aid of a new Bibles' fund.

Mr Harry, sitting at his desk, his back to a wall, likewise was busy, editing stories as fast as he could and sending them to the caseroom to be set in type.

Evening came. A first day almost over. The final stories. We drank cups of tea and the reporter Rowland Joynson broke a thick potted meat sandwich into two and insisted on handing half to me with two of his biscuits.

"You can bring your own tomorrow."

Later at Rowland's suggestion I took the editor a mug of tea.

"Well?" Mr Watson gave a tired smile across his desk.

"It's great, thank you."

"We'll make a reporter of you. Now, time you went."

But I asked could I stay on a bit longer. There was something I wanted to see.

Back in Reporters, more tea, more talk, less pressure now. Compared with other newspapers the *Observer* definitely looked old-fashioned. Its name in full was *The Accrington Observer and Times,* but everyone used the shorter name and that was its current masthead. I went through the files. Advertisements filled the front page of the main Saturday edition. Houses for sale, dances, a missing dog called Bowser, dates of council meetings and bold items like WAKE UP YOUR LIVER BILE. But Tuesday's issue, out tomorrow, would have news on the front page, a thinner affair, altogether more lively looking.

I got hold of the giant dictionary and looked up Wazygoose. It meant a printers' outing.

Heavy rumbling sounded deep down in the building.

Mr Harry glanced across at my desk and nodded. I went down the back staircase to the machine room. It was dominated by a large Rotary press and the printers were busy doing a test run. Yards of newsprint snaked slowly over rollers and drums. Printers whipped out copies as the first of the new issue appeared. They examined them, adjusted the ink flow, examined several more, someone gave a final signal of approval and the press began to increase speed. The clatter became a steady whine, the whine turned into a roar and newspapers poured from the machine.

I walked up the dark street, tomorrow's *Observer* under my arm, the ink hardly dry. I could not have felt happier.

3. Off to Court

Tuesday, first thing, still raining and cold. Autumn cold. The office, compared with the previous day's frantic rush, at first was oddly quiet, a kind of vacuum. Everyone seemed to be sitting around drinking tea and reading the Tuesday edition. A start soon on Saturday's paper, but for a few moments, tea. As an act of kindness to the plant world, I watered the geranium and decided it was living off cigarette ash and tea leaves.

I looked through the paper again (you just do at first) and found the short pieces I had written up. They were scattered on different pages and seemed to amount to very little compared with everyone else's output. A couple of pars had landed in a *Round and About Accrington* column. How could they have taken me so long? I kept it quiet, but secretly I cut out the tiny *Scouts' Social* and put it in my wallet. I'd send it to my baker friend and tell him it was my first news story.

Mr Watson bobbed his head round the door.

"Allan, take Irvine along with you to court, will you? Show him the ropes. Give him a bit of experience."

Allan Lambert was the senior reporter. It did not seem cold but he was sitting at his desk wearing a faded tweed overcoat and an old grey scarf. He was unobtrusive, the kind of man who could mingle unnoticed in a crowd.

He nodded agreeably. "Got a notebook?"

He put on his trilby.

The editor turned to me. "We'll use Allan's report this time, but write your own version and let me look at it. It'll give you a chance to practise your shorthand."

We left the office by a back door. It let into a short road, a discreet exit, with a pub at the top, and we turned into the main street, Blackburn Road. The town was bustling with vehicles and people. Lorries loaded with acid vats rumbled by. Mill machinery, furniture vans, and foodstuffs - the vehicles crawled along the choked main street vying with double-decker corporation buses for space to manoeuvre. A cotton town, industrial, with a long history of spinning and weaving.

We walked along a busy pavement past shops, grey buildings, past an occasional brash sales poster; the solid town hall in sight, the solid market hall a bit further on; we walked until Mr Lambert disappeared into a doorway and I found we were in a noisy café, Redman's.

"Just a quick cuppa before we start!"

Moments later we were joined by the reporter called Billington. "Time for a quick cuppa," he said with a pale smile. We stood at the counter drinking Redman's tea.

The magistrates' court was at the far end of the town. We sat in the box reserved for the press and listened to a drunk-in-charge case. He was a sad, thin looking man, a former soldier who had been out in the Far East. His mother stood up in the court, her hands clasped together and spoke on his behalf, saying he was not a bad lad but was unwell nowadays, ever since he had been fighting the Japanese in Burma.

Her son stood unsmiling, a crumpled figure.

Allan Lambert had warned me that the magistrates' clerk was notoriously deaf.

The clerk turned abruptly to the woman: "You say he's *what?*" He stared hard through his glasses. "*Fighting the Japs in Burnley?*"

Sniggers filled the court. The chief magistrate called sharply for silence. The mistake was explained. The man was let off with a caution.

My Pitman's shorthand was dismally slow. Allan Lambert got everything down in his notebook, even the sniggers. I determined to practice every night and become proficient.

4. Forty Cups a Day

Gradually I got to know the editor a little better. Mr Watson sat at his desk and often looked up at you over the top of his glasses when he spoke. He drank endless mugs of tea and his office was full of empty cups and mugs, some on the windowsill with mould growing in them. Forty cups of tea a day: the office joke.

He smoked frequently and from time to time beat ash off his chalk-stripe suit. It was his demobilisation suit, one given to members of the armed forces once the 1939-45 War was over.

During my second week he called me in: "There's something I need you to do, but discretely, if you will. Would you empty this lot into the bins downstairs? I don't want the wife to see it."

The ashtray was full of cigarette stubs. "If you keep it emptied from time to time?"

I didn't know why he asked me to do it, perhaps because I was new. I promised I would.

"And don't you start. Asthma and cigarettes don't mix."

But he continued to smoke.

His pill cupboard, as he called it, stood in a corner full of bottles of medicine and pills which he had bought down the years as possible cures for asthma. Among them was a bottle of Dodo tablets, a *cure* I had once tried myself, though with a feeling that anything that was named after an extinct flightless bird might not work.

Alas, Mr Watson's breathing remained uncured, and he continued to wheeze, though his optimism had not waned and I was sent to a chemist shop a couple of times to buy him the latest asthma cure as it arrived on the market.

If the editor could sometimes look frail, there was nothing weak about his ability to run the paper. Week by week he designed many of the page layouts, wrote the gossip column, *Observ(er)ations* (an old pun) and much else, crouching over his desk, a mug of tea at his right hand. When it came to writing he could be quite hard-hitting, and at times straight laced.

The reporters' room – *Reporters* - was opposite Mr Watson's door. The assistant editor, Mr Harry, sat at a desk heaped with papers, his eyes mostly looking down, scanning news stories, forever busy, answering the phone, editing, designing page layouts. He was a member of the Crossley family who owned the paper.

I learned several things about Mr Harry: one could always talk to him: he listened. And he liked a pint of beer and had a wry sense of humour.

He pointed to the office dictionary. It was a giant of a book with a shabby leather cover, seemingly rebound several times down the years. Mr Harry grinned: "No matter how you drop this thing on the desk it opens where the word *prostitute* appears. You'd think there was a secret spring!"

Several of us had tried it for ourselves and most of the time it did just as he said.

Close by, sitting at another desk in a central position which was equally loaded with paper and files, was Frank Kitchener, the sports editor. He was not exactly fat, more a bit of a podgy man with a faintly calculating smile and dark-framed glasses. In his own way he was kind and was definitely good at listening in to everything that was going on. He had a dark suit, and seemed to wear it most of the time, even when typing. His black thinning hair was plastered down with a heavy dose of Brylcreem, leaving a distinct white centre parting. Under his pen name, given the credit line *Jason's Sports Searchlight*, he wrote up the town's football team, Accrington Stanley, earning lineage by phoning match reports to some of the daily newspapers. Rowland thought he got 2d a line. His output was considerable, writing the weekend soccer matches swiftly with much pounding on his typewriter. As well as his *Observer* job he or his wife were said to have a shop of their own. Frank, who was always full of himself, had his good side, though office gossip had it that despite varying views he was aware he was always right.

If Frank listened into everything, Allan was the opposite, restrained, in his late fifties, a quiet manner.

Allan's great strength was his accurate shorthand. He was the *Observer's* best court reporter, missing nothing, even in complex cases. His shorthand was not the generally known Pitman's, but one I hadn't heard of, Sloan-Duployan. Unlike my Pitman's, he joined up his shorthand. The words trailed across each page of his notebook in long strings.

It was a surprise to learn that Allan had only one eye. The other was glass, something his spectacles concealed most of the time. Unlike the other reporters, he did not use a typewriter, but wrote up the court cases in longhand, and each word, just like his shorthand, he joined up to the next in one long string. The linotype men in the caseroom, always good for a grumble, sometimes justifiably, had given up protesting long ago and instead had learned to read his writing and didn't seem to get much wrong.

Reporting was only one side of Allan's life. His passion for music was the other.

The editor put his head round the door. "Where's Allan?" he demanded.

But Allan was not there.

Mr Watson frowned. "He'll be on a piano again! Someone go and find him!"

Someone was delegated to go round the pubs and clubs to look. Allan played anywhere where there was a handy piano. It happened again days later and it was my turn to look. There were several pubs with pianos and I failed to find him.

Mr Watson blew through his lips in exasperation when I returned. "Try Oak Street Congregational church... No, wait, try the Swedenborgian one. I'll have his ears off him when he gets back."

I had not heard of the Swedenborgians but it was only a short walk to their church. And yes,

Allan was there. The church, large, cold and empty, a mass of seats, was booming with organ music. He was huddled at the keyboard high up in the organ seat, encased in his tweed overcoat, his hat beside him, oblivious to the world. I told him what Mr Watson had said, and I got a smile.

"Tom's not musical," he said.

It was his custom at times to sit at his desk writing up news stories while still wearing his overcoat and scarf, as if it were about to rain indoors. Similarly from time to time so did the reporter, Rowland Joynson, who wore a long dark raincoat.

5. Part of the Community

Rowland, probably in his forties, hard to say, was kindness itself, and deaf. He became near enough in a panic when he couldn't hear something on the telephone. He had a deaf aid in a box on the front of his chest but kept getting it tangled. I suspected he also relied a little on lip reading when people spoke softly. He groaned when it was his turn to do the morning ringaround. He huddled over the telephone in a corner of Reporters and worked down a list pinned to the wall, phoning the police, the ambulance station, the fire brigade, and other contacts, asking if anything had happened overnight, if there were any stories.

Some mornings proved worse than others.

"Hello, police? *Observer* here. Are there any courts today? There are. What time are they? No? There aren't! Hello. Yes. Hello. There aren't any courts. Oh, there's been a crash. A car? Not a car. Two cars. Where? Sorry, *where?* Burnley? Oh, not Burnley. Were they

Accrington people? Sorry... will you wait a moment?"

He turned desperately to the rest of the room. "See what he says will you?"

Despite his deafness, Rowland was a good reporter. He was always finding news stories, especially from his district patch, the little town of Clayton-le-Moors, a couple of miles north of Accrington, trudging round it each week on the hunt. Everyone there knew Rowland. Everyone, it seemed, told him if anything newsworthy was happening. He was local, trusted, a part of the community.

He wrote historical articles, especially about Accrington, and longed to write a book. He got out the giant bound volumes of old *Observers*, stacked them on a table, and thumbed through them page by page, writing up a *Backward Glance* column for the paper. He was always being told off for not putting the volumes away.

When I asked Rowland about Swedenborgians he smiled happily. The moment we first met he had jocularly described himself as a member of the Society for the Propagation of Useless Knowledge.

And so: "Swedenborgians, they're a sort of mystical, spiritual movement. Accrington once had more Swedenborgians than anywhere else in the country. I'll bring you a book so you can read about them."

"Is Allan a Swedenborgian?"

That amused him. "Never. But I think Allan might have procured his own key to the church organ. We don't exactly ask."

Rowland's useless knowledge included numerous gems: Local people were especially proud of the town's long link with the spinning and weaving of cotton; proud, too, of Accrington Stanley football team; and they were proud, strange though it might seem at first, they were proud of a brick.

The Nori (iron) brick was made locally and was well named. It was the densest, hardest brick in the whole world. The claim was often made, but no one disagreed.

"They used them when they were building the Empire State Building," Rowland declared. "And they used them to build the foundations of Blackpool Tower."

What about Accrington Stanley? Rowland's face seemed to stiffen. He was not a soccer man. "Better ask Frank when he manages to stop typing. All I can say is they were one of the founders of the Football League. But I'll bring you a book so you can read about them."

These matters aside, there was also Howard and Bullough, cotton textile machine makers. An amazing firm. It was once the major power loom maker in the world, with almost 6,000 workers.

"Not that many today, of course."

He paused and gave a whimsical smile.

I guessed what was coming. "Don't tell me, you've got a book about it."

"As a matter of fact, I have."

I liked Rowland. There was an air of innocence about him that was engaging. And he seemed to have books on just about anything to do with Accrington and East Lancashire. A real historian, if a little odd at times. It was not unusual to see him rubbing the back of his neck vigorously when he was sitting at his desk, until the veins almost stood out on his forehead. In one way or another it was beginning to seem that there were one or two eccentrics working for the *Observer.*

Winter intensified. It was growing colder and often raining heavily. The little town seemed to grow a bit greyer each day. There wasn't one of us in the office who escaped being soaked.

Rowland peered at my shoes and tutted with concern. "You must keep your feet dry in this job. You must get a pair of these."

I almost laughed but stopped in time. His own shoes were embraced in a giant pair of black rubbery galoshes. They were overwhelming and comical. But the bad weather did not improve and a week later, a week of trudging through downpours, it was easy to appreciate how right he was and I bought a pair at a little shop in the town centre.

The moment I stretched the galoshes over my shoes my feet became enormous. I did a trial walk wearing these potty looking overshoes, which is what they were, and flop, flop, flopped along the *Observer's* bare board corridors. For some strange reason I felt like a duck. The women in the front office laughed when they saw me coming, though why I should look any funnier than Rowland I could not imagine. But the overshoes worked. Trailing round Accrington in the rain my feet now stayed dry.

Rowland might seem a shade old fashioned but more than anything he was a caring man. We were heading into the town centre and chanced on a man struggling in the road. It was a chimney sweep, hands and face black with soot. He was on a bicycle, or rather he was less on the machine and more through it, for he was giddily drunk. One leg was under the crossbar and he was struggling to stand up, and failing. Passing folk were laughing as he tried to get onto the saddle, his brooms and rods tumbling about him.

"He'll get run over!" cried Rowland.

Hardly stopping to look, he scampered out into the road as car horns blared and he grabbed the sweep by an arm. Ignoring the man's protests, he towed him and the bike to the pavement as a policeman arrived at a run. Somehow we gathered up most of the rods and brush heads before they disappeared under car wheels.

I had a bus to catch and didn't hear what happened until later. Rowland had taken charge of the bike and wheeled it back to the office. The sweep was escorted home by the constable.

"Will he be charged?"

"No, I don't think so." Rowland shook his head. "As it happens I know the constable. The problem is we're lumbered now with the man's brushes and his bike."

They were stored downstairs in a corner of the machine room. We heard that a young lad collected them later, though we never saw him.

6. Why Write?

While Mr Watson and Frank Kitchener wrote up most of the sport each week, there was a third person who enjoyed sports' writing, and that was Vic Throup.

Vic's greatest strength was cricket. He longed for the cricket season. When it came he would write entertaining descriptive pieces week after week. The more sarcastic printers in the caseroom remarked sardonically that Vic wrote up cricket matches without ever going to a cricket match, but printers say things like that. He seemed to go to matches often enough. He was in his middle to late fifties. He sat at his desk in a crumpled suit; a bit overweight, hammering away on his tank-like Royal. Like Mr Harry he liked his pint of beer, in fact he liked two, or even three.

He had been a national man, working out of Manchester, but somehow he had landed on the *Observer*. He was said to be the son of a former mayor of the town of Nelson, or perhaps Burnley some said, but he shied away from the subject if ever it were mentioned and there was no knowing if it were true. It didn't matter, he certainly knew how to write a sharp factual story, and from time to time he skimmed my work and suggested improvements.

"Get to the heart of the story!" he urged. "Find the nub of it. And check everything."

We were in Redman's cafe. Vic, unusually for him, was remarking how he had once won an essay competition, and got a job on a local weekly, before landing in Manchester.

"Why does anyone write? You just do. It's your life. That and beer! How about you?"

There wasn't a lot to say. I wrote some short poems when I was seven, filling an exercise book, and a visiting aunt announced enthusiastically that she was going to show them to a publisher, and I didn't see the poems again.

Every Saturday an old woman sat on a chair outside Blackpool's main bus station, selling the local paper. She was there, even in the rain, heavily wrapped in coats, her papers under a canvas shelter. I was in my teens and wrote an article about her for the Blackpool *Gazette and Herald*, about how she braved the weather. They paid a guinea and excited I bought a small Oxford dictionary. From that moment I knew I wanted to be a reporter, a writer. I kept that little book with me in my pocket like some people carry a wallet and I began to write in earnest. A magazine, *London Opinion*, published a short story and I saved their cheque towards a heavy coat. Part of another short story was praised in *John o' London's* magazine.

"And now we are both working for the Accy Ob!" said Vic.

I hoped it was good for him too. He never quite said.

7. An Awkward Beggar

Come another Monday morning, and the news-gathering rush was on all over again. The evening deadline was in everyone's mind. Reporters resounded to the clatter and ding of typewriters. Rowland was struggling on the phone; Mr Harry was sorting a heap of funeral reports.

"Everybody seems to be dying," he said, handing me a fistful of obituary forms. "Write these up, and make sure you mention the undertakers at the end."

The forms were sent out by the office staff the moment a death notice appeared in the paper. They asked:

Mr, Mrs or Miss; the full name and address; date of death, age, employment history, time served at different companies. Was the deceased a member of any clubs, churches or organisations? If so, which? Hobbies and interests. Leaves family of...

The date of the funeral, and more.

The forms were filled in by the undertakers, and the reporters wrote the details into readable paragraphs. In return for this information the reports printed in the paper always ended with the funeral director's name, usually *Scales Funeral Parlour had charge of the arrangements*. Scales seemed to have cornered the market, if that was the right expression.

The funerals written up, next a talk at a woman's institute on *How to Iron a Wedding Dress;* then rewriting a car-crash story lifted from the Blackburn evening paper, the *Northern Daily Telegraph,* followed by another string of small items, including a stolen dustbin.

"'A dustbin?" said Frank Kitchener, chiming in. "What crackpot would go and steal a dustbin?"

"A dustbin thief."

"Don't be sarky. Why would anyone steal one?"

"To put dust in."

"You'd think they'd pinch something better than a dustbin," persisted Frank, narked.

A busy day, and everything all right.

Less all right was Harold Taylor. Harold was the *Observer*'s key man in the small town of Haslingden, five or so miles out of Accrington, where he ruled his own little empire. Everyone in Reporters agreed that Harold was a first-class journalist, he constantly found good hard-news stories and they were always well written, but his unsmiling manner did not endear him to everyone. He had a reputation of being an awkward beggar (some used another word) and apparently young trainee reporters had a hard time working with him.

The first time we met it was also obvious he did not like me. By chance I had written up a story from the hamlet of Baxenden and Harold glared, saying that Baxenden was *his* territory and he had planned to do the same story for long enough. I nearly said then why hadn't he?

I mentioned that Harold didn't like me, and was told that Harold didn't like anybody in particular. If you didn't do everything at 103 per cent then you weren't a friend of Harold's.

His office in Haslingden was at the top of two or three flights of stairs and several in Reporters smirked the day they heard that Harold and a visiting journalist had had a row. Both men were tall and the visitor had said: "Any more of this and I'll knock you down the bloody stairs."

Apparently it put Harold in his place for a while.

Essentially he was a distant figure, and kept himself to himself. But there was another side to the man. A few wondered why such a skilled reporter was working for a small local paper like the *Observer*. Vic somehow gleaned over a pint of beer that Harold during the 1939-45

War – which had ended only five years earlier - had served on the dreaded Arctic convoys, carrying weapons to Russia, at times through bitter winter blizzards. Harold had experienced a hard war and he suffered from nervous bouts. The war might explain Harold.

There was one woman reporter at the *Observer*. She wrote under the name of Geraldine. She sat at her desk, big bosomed, a shawl round her shoulders, hammering on a typewriter, an appraising expression, too busy to talk.

At first I thought Geraldine was her real name, but apparently not. She was related to the Crossley family and wrote the woman's column, *Ladies' Chain,* and did the fashion page. She was also the paper's feared drama critic, reviewing plays staged by the local amateur dramatic societies, but especially by Accrington Arts Club. She was a sharp, acerbic reviewer, and caused angry outcries, particularly the day she wrote that the programme should have billed the play's sturdy-voiced prompt as one of the actors.

Geraldine's reputation aside, beyond *Good morning* or *Hello* we never really conversed and I never got to know her. She simply smiled and retreated into herself.

The *Observer* had no staff photographer. Instead a freelance, Garth Dawson, took the pictures. He was about twenty-six years old, fair-haired and had a quiet smile. He photographed just about everything and anything that was going on in the *Observer's* circulation area. He had been doing work for the paper for about a year when we met and he was good to work with.

We were drinking a cup of tea.

"Before I worked for the *Observer* I pedalled round town on a bike. I'd a folding camera and started taking pictures of church processions. Especially at Whit. The town's full of church processions at Whit. I put the photos in the window at my dad's shoe and repair shop and people bought copies.

"Thing was, I kept meeting Mr Harry at the processions – it was when he was a reporter – and he asked if I could help. Well, I said yes!"

Garth had graduated to a small car. Each week Mr Watson, Mr Harry and Frank would sort out what to cover: and Garth was called in to take the pictures: car crashes, club meetings, Accrington Stanley soccer matches, whatever.

I liked Garth. He started his own photographers, renting an empty shop. Later he changed his place of work to a brown wooden-walled shed in the town centre. Single storey, his modest photographer's studio lay a short distance from the parish church and he did well.

8. Lodgings

A week in an hotel, then a day off to find cheaper lodgings. An advertisement in a shop window led me half way up the valley side to a smoky street of gardenless houses and Mrs Bailey's B and B. I stepped straight off the sandstone pavement into a narrow passage.

She took me upstairs into the front bedroom.

"Best room in t'house," said Mrs Bailey. She clasped hefty hands over her apron.

"How much did you say?" I asked again.

"Take it or leave it, twenty-five shillings a week."

Twenty-five shillings was just about affordable. Green painted walls, a cream painted ceiling, in one corner a big bed with (as I discovered) noisy springs; and in the other a blue and white Victorian water jug and basin on a marble topped stand. I stared at the last in disbelief recalling that the last one I had seen had been in a junk shop.

"You'll not find many places as good as this," Mrs Bailey assured me.

For the moment I took it.

At six-thirty each morning a clatter of boots and clogs on the pavement below the window signalled passing spinners and weavers on their way to a mill. At five to seven voices and more boots, a stream of factory workers; at seven-thirty a hooter blasting somewhere nearby; at twenty to eight a horse and cart and the clatter of milk bottles. Each morning I surrendered and got dressed.

For company, Mrs Bailey's seven-year-old son stood alongside at the breakfast table, his unwiped nose hovering at the edge. Silent and solemn eyed, he watched as I ate a heap of fried potatoes and bacon, a blob of snot hanging ready to drop.

For three mornings I tolerated this snitch of a kid but finally I had had enough and told him to go or I'd wallop him. But he didn't go, watching every mouthful, and in desperation I grabbed a spoon and whacked him on the head.

"Scram!" I told him.

Five minutes later his mother pushed me out of the front door, my case landing on the pavement beside me.

I went to work wondering why ever I had come to this gloomy industrial town. Perhaps the lad was simply hungry. Sizeable breakfasts were probably reserved for paying guests. But it didn't make me feel any better.

"So what are you so happy about?"

Frank Kitchener looked across Reporters.

"It's my digs."

I told him about the best room, and the twanging bed, but mostly the snot.

"What you ought to do," said Frank, "is talk to Allan."

Before I fully appreciated my good luck, Allan Lambert had taken me along to his home for lunch and introduced me to his wife Edith.

She was cheerful, intelligent, fond of music, wore a pinny, and her greying hair tied in a small bun. "We're used to the wild ways of reporters," she said with a laugh. "You'd better stay with us."

I moved in the same day, hoping to stay a week or so while looking for another B and B; in fact I was to stay for more than two years.

The Lamberts lived in Sandy Lane and their home was warm and friendly, full of unexpected callers and lots of music.

"Come in to the front room," Allan said. "I've something I want you to hear."

Almost a quarter of the tiny parlour was occupied by a grand piano, a beautiful Bechstein. Allan sat at the keyboard, a solid figure with magical fingers, self-taught and not perhaps the world's best pianist, but skilled enough. Within seconds Chopin flowed through him like a river. It was marvellous. Allan smoked a cigarette as he thundered away on the keys and the ash grew and grew and hung down in a long drooping curve, which astonishingly remained intact, unbroken, until the last flourish on the keyboard, and only then did the ash break off and disappear into the keys.

"Now listen to this." And he was off again, another cigarette, pouring out Liszt's *Mephisto Valse.*

"Wonderful," said Allan enthusiastically. "Full of thunder."

Full of ash, too. When Edith finally persuaded Allan to get a man in to clean the piano no one was surprised to find a thick layer of cigarette ash lay under the keys.

As I heard later, if Allan played a piece of music that he didn't quite know, he *approximated* it. The result would not suit purists but to many of us it was greatly enjoyable. Sometimes Allan's friend Ernest Atkinson from higher up Sandy Lane would join him. Then the two men would share the keyboard sitting side by side, both of them oblivious to the world around them, working inventively through a series of duets.

It did not matter how cold the days were now, or how rain swept the hills and poured down into the solid little town, at the Lamberts' there was warmth and music, especially on Sunday evenings. Guests, sometimes musicians, arrived and squeezed into the front parlour. Tall stories were told, Allan played the piano, cups of tea were brought in. It was a musical home.

"Didn't I tell you?" said Frank.

"Thank you, you did," I told him, gratefully. Frank had done more than find me digs, he had found me a family.

9. Fire!

It was four in the afternoon and already dark. I had been sent to interview a golden wedding couple out at the little village of Huncoat on Accrington's outskirts, and tomorrow Garth would go and take their photograph. A matter now of - *Who, what, where, when, why?* - the order varying, but often the simple basis of a news story.

Mr and Mrs Whalley. A Lancashire couple. He'd worked in a butcher's; she had brought up the children. Mr Whalley did most of the talking.

"Mary and me, we met up at Baxenden and we took a steamer trip to the Isle of Man. It was special, for me anyway. Never been before, neither on us. Course we'd known each other long enough for me to ask. But I hadn't, not yet. Well, it wasn't that easy because the old boat was that full and nowhere to sit on our own, so we had to sit on deck on a kipper box and that's where I proposed."

On a kipper box?

They both laughed. "It was empty but it whiffed a bit."

It was an obvious question. "Do you like kippers?"

His eyes lit. "Aye, if they're Manx uns!"

He had probably said that a few times down the years.

Back at the *Observer* I wrote it up. The golden wedding made eight pars.

I left by the back door and walked up to Blackburn Road. Mr Watson still had a light burning, still at his desk, still at work.

The town centre was gloomy, lit by a few street lights, another dank November night, and I set off to Allan's and supper. I was crossing Blackburn Road into Church Street as an odd flicker of light made me pause. It seemed to come from a large corner ironmonger's shop called Bridge's. A moment later my senses were racing. The building had three stories and the first-floor windows were full of flames.

Ring the fire brigade first - or the Observer? It seemed silly later even to have had such a thought. Madly I ran to a phone box and called the brigade; then I rang the office and got Mr Watson.

But others inside the building had called the brigade as well and soon fire engines screeched to a halt in front of the shop. A crowd gathered. The flames were increasing.

The fire raged for more than an hour, spreading to the second and third floors at the front of the building. Flames swept through rooms, shattering windows. Streams of plate glass and glowing debris came crashing into the street and the gaping windows revealed an inferno. Fittings could be seen breaking away from the walls and ceilings.

It was a pure fluke. I stood in a doorway facing the shop as a man next to me started saying how he had discovered the fire. I reached for my notebook. He told me how he and other members of the staff had been inside stocktaking.

"We heard something falling and I went to look what it was. I saw a glow from the stairs. Flames were round the stairs and the lift-housing shaft."

They had raced to use the shop's hose and extinguishers and someone called the brigade.

For me it was a lucky break and I scribbled furiously. Mr Watson arrived wrapped in his overcoat, his trilby pulled well down, and I told him what the shop man had said. He looked sharply into the crowd. "Try and keep it quiet. The *Telegraph* man's here." He was, and he had heard. The reporter began to question the shop worker.

Back at the office, I sat at the typewriter my mind suddenly blank. I was over excited and struggling to get started. Mr Watson came in and read the first half page. He said little for a while then he suggested parts that could be written a bit differently, and gradually, though he only seemed to look on for a short time, the essentials were written and somehow, as I realised more fully later, he generously let it seem as if I had written the whole thing by myself.

"It's a good story," he said, shuffling and rereading the pages of copy.

I told him how I had not known whether to ring him first, or whether to ring the fire brigade.

"You should have phoned the photographer first."

Next day, press day, experienced Vic took over. He phoned Bridge's management and after initial hesitation on their part he encouraged them to estimate the approximate damage. He updated the intro, added in details from the fire brigade: twenty firemen had fought the blaze; part of a roof had collapsed; at its peak flames had poured from twenty or more windows, but the firemen had done what had seemed impossible, they had saved the main building.

Garth arrived with pictures of firemen clambering over the shop's roof and another man high up on a turntable ladder directing a hosepipe into the burning building. J W Bridge Ltd would survive.

Saturday's splash story spread across seven columns:

FIRE HAVOC IN ACCRINGTON

Crowds watch town-

centre blaze

£15,000 to £20,000

damage estimate.

An exciting week.

10. Essentials

I took a cup of tea into Mr Watson. A few days had passed since the fire. He wanted to know how I liked living at Allan's, and did I enjoy music; did I know that Allan's family, the Lamberts, were connected with a famous cricket bat firm over at the town of Nelson, and what did I think of Accrington now I'd had time to see it? He went on about Accrington Stanley, how they were a bit shaky this season, about their chances. He talked about his own early days as a reporter, working for the *East Lancashire Sentinel,* before he joined the *Observer* as a journalist, and later became the editor. He stressed how he hoped to increase the *Observer's* news coverage; and how he had started writing... making it a practice to count the number of words in each news story, and then cutting out as many as he could before handing it in. Making it taut, no padding.

"I prefer short words. *Start* and *begin,* never *commence.* Use Anglo-Saxon words if possible.

And no so-called poetic words: use *among* not *amongst,* and *while* not *whilst.* And short sentences."

Later I learned more about writing short news sentences. Twenty-five to thirty words to a paragraph, one sentence wherever possible, though letting it run if cutting would destroy the sense. It proved to be a hard discipline.

"One clear thought to each sentence."

On page layouts, he favoured modest headlines.

"Let the story speak for itself. Avoid screamers. We're not the *Mirror.*"

We talked about the *Observer* building. It had an engaging old-fashioned feel about it, worn corridors and little rooms, not exactly shabby, but as if many small dramas had taken place there. And I guessed that some had. Dickens would have appreciated the *Observer* and its toiling reporters and printers. It was no surprise to learn that over the years the rambling building one way or another had absorbed a complete house, a garage and even stables which had held carriage horses.

"And now, a newspaper!"

He was all right was Mr Watson. Essentials. A lesson, without it seeming like a lesson. Generously he had made a still green cub reporter feel he had written the Bridge's fire story by himself, though of course I knew I hadn't, and I was well aware too of Vic's help, again generously giving me most of the credit. It was a good feeling.

11. Shorthand Challenge

A December Monday. A bitter wind was blowing and snow was forecast. I began looking into shop windows at the price of overcoats.

A heavy stamping of boots echoed on the *Observer*'s back staircase and a lean-faced man disappeared into the editor's office. Angry voices sounded. In Reporters typewriters fell silent as snatches of conversation sounded across the corridor.

Fred Billington brought in short reports. "It's gasbags. He's on about his speech at last week's highway's committee. He says we got it wrong."

Groans sounded. Everyone knew the councillor: a well-meaning, strong-minded socialist, fond of his own voice.

The door opened and Mr Watson looked in. His face was expressionless. "Allan, come in will you?"

With Allan in the editor's office the row went on. Then a door banged and heavy steps sounded in the corridor as the councillor left.

Mr Watson, Allan and Mr Harry came into Reporters looking grim faced. "He means well," said the editor, "but there's little wonder we got him wrong. It was a muddle. There was no way we could print it the way he said it."

We sat at our desks and listened as Allan read out his notes for a second time and compared them with the version in the paper. The editor and Mr Harry were satisfied; the councillor had been ambiguous.

Mr Watson took off his glasses and wiped them with the edge of his cardigan. "All right. We'll do exactly as he demands. Allan, at the next meeting I don't want you to summarise. Take down everything. If he wants us to report exactly as he says, then that's exactly what we'll do."

"It could cause us a lot of trouble," put in Frank.

"We'll still do it," said Mr Watson.

A week later at a full council meeting Allan's shorthand was given its most strenuous test in his forty years as a journalist. Mr Watson designated Vic to do the first take, and Allan the second. But should the complaining councillor get up to speak earlier, then Allan would take over from Vic. Vic's shorthand was good, but Allan's was better.

The day of the meeting arrived. Mr Harry sent me along to sit in for experience, and for fun I began to make a few notes of my own – the humorous asides, the council chamber's fans failing to dispel the hot air; the empty tea cups concealed behind the town clerk's desk; the councillor who dozed off from time to time, only to wake up with a start.

Not that the chamber was quiet. An angry row began between Conservative and Labour members about the cost of road repairs.

The complaining councillor stood up to speak. He went on at some length and Allan took down everything, every word, every cough, all the *ums*, all the *ers,* anything that he said twice.

He wrote it up at home that evening, leaning on his Bechstein. Allan had missed nothing. He knew the councillor was going to be upset.

"You know, Tom," said Allan next morning as he handed in his copy. "I feel sorry for the man."

"He's not a bad man," said Rowland. "I know he does a lot of good and he visits sick folk."

Mr Watson scanned the first few pages. "He's the one who's insisted on this, not us. But we'll not use it all."

The story was several sheets long. In the end only a few paragraphs went in along with the bit I had done.

It was a Saturday morning and a few flakes of snow were falling. The councillor climbed the steps once more. He stamped less heavily this time and there were no angry shouts from the editor's office. When the man left three-quarters of an hour later he and Mr Watson had been drinking tea (made by Mr Harry, no less) and we were told it had ended with handshakes.

"He's agreed to let us edit his speeches," said Mr Watson. "We'll still give him plenty of cover."

Peace again.

12. Christmas

The indoor jobs – courts, council meetings, divisional health sessions, inquests – were much preferred now to tramping round the districts in the cold hunting for news.

It was back to writing up football reports. The local teams. Factories, working men's clubs, schools - if they had a soccer team then the office sent them a questionnaire and asked them to fill it in.

Team A: Please print all names in full, or include initials.

Team B: ditto. What was the score?

Referee's comments, if any.

Our job was to turn their notes into readable stories.

Some referee's comments were vividly vulgar. Others made a real attempt at describing what had happened. A favourite was the day a team beat a rival team by ten goals to nil.

They was never in the pictures, affirmed the referee.

Worsening weather intervened and some matches were cancelled. A cruel wind blew down off the hills and swept into the town. Its tortured song entered through keyholes. Wild gusts slammed the sides of houses, ripped slates off roofs, sent a house chimney toppling in Whalley Road. A gale story was looming and I was given charge of welding the incidents into a double-column piece. Nor did any of us have far to go to be involved.

Allan and I were struggling home to Sandy Lane, heads down, going for lunch, when a canvas-topped stall outside the market hall lifted up off the cobbles and sailed across the road. It crashed in a tangle of wood, feet away from an old woman. We hurried to her side and helped her into the market hall where she sat and Allan got her a hot drink. She was badly shocked but uninjured and eventually Allan insisted on walking with her up to her home in up Avenue Parade.

The woman's lucky escape made the intro and I hammered it out on my Underwood.

Almost Christmas. I carried in a steaming mug of tea and set it down on Mr Watson's desk. Extra sugar. He shuffled aside a heap of papers.

"I've been reading your weather round-up. It's good as far as it goes, but it's a bit wordy. I've crossed a few out."

I read his deletions. He was right. Too wordy.

He said again how he preferred short words to long ones, this despite Allan's frequent jest: *Never use a short word if a long one will do!*

"You're not the only one. Worse things can happen. Headlines can be a real problem. I wrote a clanger soon after I started as editor: *Police probe dead woman.*"

He reached for his tea. "Now you know why I ban *probe* in headings."

A day or so later he startled Reporters, putting his head round the door, and demanding: "Who's been ringing New York?"

New York? The thought was almost astonishing. That anyone at the *Observer* dared to make an expensive 3,000-mile telephone call to America sounded almost unreal. But the call was shown on the phone bill. No one as far as I heard owned up and if the accounts staff ever found out who made it, we were never told. We blamed Harold Taylor.

Christmas at the Lamberts. We hugged the fireside, had turkey for dinner, drank hot toddy, and listened to the Queen's speech on the radio. Snow had been predicted and overnight the wind increased. By dawn a blizzard was raging.

Traffic chaos stories took over the paper: ambulances struggled to get to the hospital;

homes were cut off; there was talk of coal rationing; council workmen were out in the worst of it, shovelling at the drifts.

In Reporters once more a greater reliance on the phone; some districts were cut off. There was always news. Blizzards are news.

13. Caseroom Disaster

Late on Friday afternoon, disaster struck in the caseroom. Mr. Harry, his face suddenly grim, quit his desk and hurried along to see what had happened. The room lay a few strides away from Reporters and we crowded after him.

The place was noisy with the clatter of Linotype machines. Time was short. The linomen were busily typing on the keyboards, turning pages of news copy into metal type. Press time was nearing and people were becoming edgy and anxious.

Two layout men in aprons were on their knees in front of a metal-topped table - known as a *stone.* They were trying to pick up a mass of type, which had tumbled across the floor.

It had happened in moments. A compositor had been making up a news page. Working to a handwritten layout, he had slotted each metal story into a *chase,* an oblong metal frame lying flat out on the table, the same size as an

Observer page. The page full, the comp had hammered the type level with a wooden block and mallet, rolled ink on and taken a page proof. The job nearly over, he tightened the page a bit more within the frame - but too much. Abruptly, the middle of the page bulged up and a mass of type tumbled over the edge.

The overseer, balding, and in his sixties, a man of few words, barked: "Save all you can!"

He stood now silently, a strong presence, watchful, as the men knelt on the boards and tried to pick up whole paragraphs. If still intact they could go back in the page and not have to be reset. But the outcome looked doubtful. Time was going.

Catching Mr Harry's anxious expression we cleared off back to Reporters.

Rowland said: "I've seen a whole page of type drop out of a *chase,* but it's the first time I've seen it spring up."

Pieing the type it was called. Either way, a printer's nightmare. Correctly tightened, a *chase* could be removed from the stone intact, the whole page safely clamped together. But too slack, and the stories dropped out. Now the opposite had happened.

The compositors saved less than half of the page. The rest had to be reset.

"Damn it!" said Mr Watson, who rarely swore.

The caseroom seemed to be a world apart from that of the reporters who were often out covering meetings and following up stories. In the caseroom a different pace and a different vocabulary existed. Men in ink-stained aprons used unfamiliar words and phrases, and cracked their own jokes, not all polite, a good many about us reporters. Words and phrases like *chase, flong, a line of lead, slugs, upper and lower cases, a stick, flatbed, line-rules, galley proofs* - old printing terms, they became part of daily vocabulary. The type in the made-up pages was all backwards until printed. It was an acquired skill, but most of us could soon read it the wrong way round, the more skilled able to spot spelling errors, even though they were backwards.

Little by little I came to know several of the caseroom men. One in particular, Guy Cunliffe, the *Observer's* proof reader. He sat in a little box-like office in a corner of the caseroom reading everything that was printed in the paper, all Tuesday's pages, all Saturday's – in fact, every news item and every advertisement. It always amazed me. Guy read and corrected it all.

Different reporters would go in to copyhold the stories and read with him. Printers' errors were marked on proofs and sent back to the lino men for correction. It was a demanding, precise job, hard on the eyes.

Guy had a notebook full of memorable items. Spelling mistakes . . .

Queueing or *queuing? All right* or *alright? Accomodation or accommodation?* (The last the most misspelled word in the English language, affirmed Guy).

The mayor, wearing the newly restored gold chain of office, passed through the open door into the council chamber. (*Passed*, rudely spelled).

Double meanings ...*the couple were at it on the bridge for a whole year* (They were painting it). The printers loved this one and stuck a copy on the door of Reporters.

Guy delighted in cricket and used to be a bowler, which was why he liked to have Vic with him as copyholder. The two of them enthused about cricketers and especially about legendary batsman Eddie Paynter who was born in Oswaldtwistle. Paynter played in seven Tests against Australia and was Guy's hero.

"In one Test he was taken to hospital with tonsillitis, really ill," said Guy. "But what did he do? He ignored all the doctors and got out of bed. Looking like death he went and batted. That's what he did! And it worked. He helped England win the Ashes!"

Guy wore glasses. "I don't really need them, even now. But when I was first here as a young man and got to be proof reader I thought I'd better save my eyes, not wear 'em out, I got glasses to keep me going, even though I was told I didn't need 'em. Best thing I ever did. Even six-point type is still no problem. I've always had good sight and could bowl a good googly or two!"

Six point type was really small and was often used for printing match results and market prices. I knew already that an inch of type measured 72 points, so six definitely was little.

14. Bring-and-Buy

Mr Harry put me down in the diary to cover a bring-and-buy sale. A Saturday afternoon job. The sky was leaden and more snow was forecast.

Every name sells a copy, I reminded myself as I arrived at the church hall armed with a notebook and a sharpened pencil.

"I'm from the *Observer*," I explained to the man taking the entrance money at the door.

The man's face lit up. "Oh, aye. Come in, lad." The doorkeeper turned to the hall where a group of women was chatting alongside lines of stalls as they waited for the opening. It seems I was expected.

"IT'S T'REPORTER FROM T'OBSERVER!" bawled the man.

This public introduction left me dying with embarrassment. Every person in the hall seemed to turn to examine "t'reporter."

"I'd just like to see the secretary," I told him discretely.

"Aye, lad. He's coming now. HE WANTS YOU, JOE!" bawled the man again.

The secretary, Joe, said they urgently needed to raise a huge sum of money, £200 to repair or even buy some new church doors, which had rotted all along the bottom edges. He was very hopeful. He said there would be another sale after this one in a month's time.

He directed me to the tearoom and I was given a cup of tea and a cherry cake and told I needn't pay, but thinking about the doors it seemed better if I did.

"Spell my name right this time," advised a hefty looking woman at the bran tub. "Mrs Margerson, with one G. That deaf man at your place wrote it with two last time."

I went round name-collecting, making sure I had them in full...

"Whatever you do, don't leave out their first names, or their initials," Mr Harry had instructed. "People look undressed without them."

... names of stallholders, the tearoom women, the Vicar, the seconder, the guest speaker, the doorman, Joe the secretary, the treasurer, the chairman, everyone. Bread and butter journalism. By this time the public had been allowed in and the gabble of voices was deafening. All however were kept waiting.

Three honoured guests and the Vicar filed onto the platform and sat down on a row of small Sunday School wooden chairs. One by one speeches of welcome followed, three "How pleased I am..."

About seventy women, armed with empty bags and baskets, waited stolidly and saved their strength. Finally the Vicar said a prayer and everyone on the platform sat back. In the moment that ensued there was a puzzled silence and the chairman stood up hurriedly.

"I declare the sale open..."

The women surged like a dam released. They swamped the stalls. Unprepared for this onslaught, I was bundled aside.

I hurried back to Sandy Lane and wrote up the bring-and-buy on top of Allan's Bechstein, ready for Monday. With all the names it would make half a column, including Mrs Margerson with one G.

Come Monday, the start of a fresh week. I was enjoying this! More bring-and-buy stories; more church bazaars; more money-raisers. Not all of the stories landed on my desk, but enough did. Outside, cold and the threat of more snow, but I decided to put off buying an overcoat for just a little longer.

Press time still a few hours away, and no one was pausing. Typewriters were clattering in bursts of activity.

The editor looked round the edge of the door. "Has the filth case come yet?"

"No. Allan's still on with it."

"It just would be a long session today of all days."

Along the corridor in the caseroom linotype machines clicked and chattered. Steel saws screamed as they carved metal slabs to match the shapes of picture blocks. Time was going.

"Anything from Allan?" The editor was back at the door, cigarette taken from his mouth.

"Nothing."

"Is our 'phone in order?"

Mr Harry found it was.

"Confound it! Where is he?"

And then the telephone rang. Allan said he was still in Preston and about to catch the train back to Accrington. The case had gone on and on. To complicate matters, his notebook was full but he would get some paper at the station and write it up on the train.

An hour later he arrived back at the office, a bit breathless and handed Mr Watson his completed copy. It was written on railway lavatory paper.

"I hadn't time to get another notebook. And I've lost my scarf."

His old grey scarf, thrown away once by Edith, but rescued by an indignant Allan. Now, gone again. For once Allan looked dismal.

The two men disappeared into the editor's office.

Mr Harry caught my eye and shuffled a paper. "Look, do this late wedding." He glanced at the photograph. "No, leave it."

The photograph, sent in by a Burnley shop, landed in a bin. "An ARP. I'll see to the write-up. Will you do the calls?"

At times now it was my turn to do the ringaround. I sat at the phone desk and began to ring down the list pinned to the wall: the police, the fire station, the ambulance, the hospital, and numerous others. There were two items, a man taken to hospital with cuts to his face after stumbling on a slippery pavement, and a child who had broken an arm at a school party.

"Quick as you can," urged Mr Harry.

My own typing was getting faster. "What's ARP?"

"Already pregnant. We won't use the picture. Tom won't allow them."

Later I learned that a photograph of a bride bulging in a white virginal wedding dress was not regarded as the *Observer's* style.

15. First Inquest

More snow engulfed the town. It began to fall soon after midnight and by morning it had turned into a fresh storm, halting traffic, making main roads and pavements almost impassable. Everyone seemed to arrive at the office coughing.

If winter was outside in the streets, inside Reporters it was unnaturally hot and no one was surprised to learn that the heating boiler was making worrying noises. Even Allan took off his overcoat. Typewriters were being hammered. Another *Observer* was slowly coming together. I caught Vic pouring a cup of cold tea on the geranium.

Mr Watson bobbed his head round the door.

"How's your shorthand? Good enough? Well there's an inquest. Go and give it a go."

I must have gulped but said I would. A first solo court story. It was progress.

He nodded. "You'll not be alone. Talk to the *Telegraph* reporter if you get stuck."

He turned to Allan. "Is your Harold in town?"

It seemed that Harold was, whoever Harold might be. Not Harold Taylor apparently. "Tell him you work here, and you'll be all right."

I went, flopping through the snow, thinking that after all I definitely would see about a warmer coat.

The inquest was an unexpectedly unpleasant experience. A constable had pointed me to the press box and for several minutes I sat alone, waiting apprehensively for it to start. Would my shorthand be good enough? I hoped so.

The inquest was about to begin as another reporter slid in. He looked frozen. I guessed that this was Harold, but there was no time to talk. We huddled in the box while we heard how a lorry driver had fallen onto a pair of scissors, and had been found dead by his wife outside the backyard lavatory. The scissors had been found stuck somehow into the man's neck. The word used by the police was *impaled;* it was weird and bloody and no details were omitted.

The other reporter looked at my drawn face as we got up to go. "Don't let it get you. Don't get involved; see it as a job. By the way, I'm Harold. Harold Hodgson. I hear you're living with Allan and Edith?"

Harold in fact was married to the Lamberts' daughter, Dorothy. He was their son-in-law.

The inquest proved to be an ordeal to write. I toned down the gruesome bits and it made a mere seven paragraphs.

16. A Hrumph

A few days later Mr Harry gave me a message. "Go along to Mr Richard's office. He wants to see you."

Puzzled, I went to the little office that lay between the printers and the telephone girls. Richard Crossley was one of the *Observer's* owners.

His office had an air of being little used. A large, polished shiny desk dominated it. Printers wanting to go to the telephonists would open the door and see if Mr Richard were sitting there, and if he wasn't they took a short cut through the office to the other side. But if he were, then they took the long route, going down a flight of stairs, along a passage under his office, and then up more stairs to the telephonists.

Mr Richard with his brother Robert owned the *Observer*. Both were probably in their middle sixties and so far I had not met either of them.

The Crossleys... the *Observer* I now knew was 60 or so years old. Started in 1887 by the Toulmin family of Preston, who had owned the *Preston Guardian* and *Blackburn Times,* apparently it was not an instant success, losing money, and they sold it to the paper's manager, Richard Shaw Crossley who bought it with £1,000 borrowed from an uncle. Later he bought out the *Times,* calling it the *Accrington Observer and Times.* The Tuesday *Observer* was started in 1900 and later Richard and Robert Crossley took over the whole thing.

I knocked on the door and went in. Mr Richard was portly and wore a voluminous grey suit and somewhat overflowed his swivel seat. He had a watchful manner and asked me to go down to his car in the back street to fetch a folder of papers. He had forgotten to bring it up.

The folder lay there and I was about to slam the door shut when I noticed something stuffed down the side of the seat. It was a wallet and, astonishingly, it was bulging with money. At a guess, there were forty or fifty pounds in notes, perhaps more.

Feeling pleased at this discovery, I took the wallet upstairs and placed it on the desk next to a cup of tea.

"I found this wallet wedged in by a seat, Mr Richard," I told him.

He stared momentarily as if he were not sure what it was, then he picked it up, and with something that sounded like *Hrumph!* he dropped it into a drawer. And that was all. Back at Reporters I wasn't even sure if he had said thank you.

Even Rowland thought it strange. "Most of the time I can't hear what the man's talking about. It was probably his brother's, Mr Robert's."

Outside it was bitterly cold and the snow-covered pavements were starting to freeze. Parts of the office, including the caseroom and Reporters, were suffering from the heating boiler's latest quirk. Heating engineers had been called back into the building which was no longer over-heated but hardly heated at all. We all sat with our coats on.

At lunchtime we retreated up the back street to the warmth of the pub. Time for a pint at the pub's fireside. Today was Vic's birthday.

Vic looked round the bar appreciatively. He always looked appreciatively when he had a pint of beer in front of him. "I reckon a good few *Observer* men have been in and out of this place over the years."

Everyone agreed.

"Just so long as you all keep coming out again, I don't mind," said Mr Watson, who treated us.

Allan, who rarely drank beer, and when he did, no more than a half-pint, and that in a sense, *wasted*, gulped his down in moments as if it were a glass of water.

His beer gone, he drifted off to examine the pub's piano (not a Bechstein), but for some unknown reason, though he had played on it often enough in the past, he found it had been jammed into a corner where he could not get it open. It was not the regular barman, so perhaps that was the reason.

We drank our beer and wished Vic a happy birthday again.

"Vic," said Allan, as we remembered we were journalists and needed to get back to work, "you must come home and have lunch with us next week. I'll play you something special."

Another copy of the *Mephisto* had arrived in the post.

17. Hippodrome Crisis

Mr Harry filled in the diary and put me down to review the week's new show at the Hippodrome Theatre. It was a Monday evening task and not every reporter wanted it. There was always a rush to write it up and get it into the next morning's paper.

The building stood in a dismal street and the theatre was struggling to keep going. So too were some of the shows.

The Red Rose Theatre group was one of the exceptions. A resident show, the young team of actors put on a different play each week. During the afternoons they rehearsed next week's play and in the evenings presented this week's production. They were a talented hard working group, frequently entertaining, and I admired their tenacity. Despite their efforts, as each week's new play opened on Mondays, which was billed as Pensioners' Night, the audience totalled little more than a couple of dozen people mostly on the front rows of the stalls, the rest of the theatre behind them yawning emptily, though audiences improved later in the week.

Mr Ross Jones, the theatre manager, phoned to say he wanted to give me "a good story". I went round to his office and sat on a dangerously creaking chair and took notes. All his office chairs seemed to creak.

He spoke boldly, how he was going to bring better shows to Accrington; good variety ones; really entertaining ones. He wanted to fill the theatre. The Hippodrome was not finished yet.

I took it all down, though noticed in passing that his navy blue suit was somehow a bit greasy round the edges of the collar and he looked tired. A bit like the Hippodrome itself.

Hardly had Mr Jones' piece appeared in the *Observer*, then came the announcement of the theatre's impending shutdown.

At once audiences improved. A Save-the-Hippodrome campaign began. A loudspeaker car drove round the town calling on the public to help, but it was not enough and the theatre closed.

Rowland said: "Everyone's wanting to watch television these days."

And money was tight. The town's engineering industry was on short-time working, adding to the gloom.

Yet the closure was temporary. Mr Jones surprised everyone and announced that the Hippodrome was going to reopen. The theatre was switching from plays to variety and revues, including 'attractive women.' Variety shows had often been better supported. The trouper comedian Frank Randle had been booked with one of his own productions, *Randle's Scandals*.

"Well at least he's a laugh," said Frank. "Mother says he swears too much but he is funny."

It seems Randle had appeared at the Hippodrome on other occasions, but this time something went wrong. Mr Watson had a tip-off that there was trouble. Randle's show, booked to open on Monday evening, had walked out on him, apparently that morning.

Mr Harry sent me round and I found a frantic Mr Jones shouting down the phone to Randle's agent, trying to book substitute acts in time for that evening.

I knew nothing about Randle, though Rowland did. "He's funny but he can be as awkward as they come."

The comedian's mischievous wit and the vulgarity of his act had already caused conflict with the police, especially in Blackpool. At times they had banned his material.

Walkout or no walkout, Randle was still coming to Accrington. By late afternoon a new line-up began to arrive in town by train and cars, including a last-minute group of dancing girls who had scarcely ten minutes on-stage to work out their routine before the first members of the audience began to take their seats.

To Mr Jones delight the audience was bigger than usual. His plan might just work. Down in the orchestra pit three musicians (possibly four, it was hard to see) struck up a lively attempt at a cheerful medley.

The long-legged girls danced on to approving whistles and when their act seemed to have concluding the music somehow did not end as expected, and the dancers failed to make their exit and found themselves dancing through their routine all over again before they were engulfed in swathes of crimson curtains. The pensioners loved them.

An acrobatic act followed; and then a big-chested singer in evening dress. His opening song *If You Were the Only Girl in the World,* went down well, and the second *Just a Song at Twilight* likewise but as he seemed set to continue the audience began to grow restive. We saw an arm waving urgently in the wings and the singer bowed out to half-hearted applause.

And now Frank Randle appeared and instantly the atmosphere changed. In moments his drunken-man act had the audience rocking with laughter. He reeled about the stage holding a Guinness beer bottle, brilliantly managing several times to avoid falling into the orchestra pit but otherwise walking headlong into props and curtains, all the while talking as he hunted for his cat. He looked under things; and round things; tried not to tread on its tail; called its name; swore at it; sounded worried.

And Randle, his jokes, not as telling in print, but typical: peering through a Potato Pie shop window where a cat was lying out full-length on top of a long pie.

Bellowing loudly: "*A, misses. Yon cat's sleeping on thee pie crust!*"

And she*: "Aye, it's all right, it likes to be near its kittens."*

We could almost see that cat when the show came to an end.

There wasn't much time but writing up the review did not seem daunting, better than that, this might present a good opportunity to get to talk with Randle himself. I might find out why his original company had walked out. It would be a good story and worth a quick try.

Mr Jones, urged on by my promises of lots of good publicity, agreed to take me into the comedian's dressing room and pretend that I was his son, though he warned me not to say I was a reporter. Randle was dead against the Press.

Other reporters were also in the theatre trying to get the story, including a man from the *Daily Express*. Mr Jones said Randle had already seen one of them off with a salvo of ripe language.

The two of us entered Randle's tiny dressing room where he was sitting in front of a mirror wiping off his grease paint. He was drinking from a generous sized bottle of whisky, lightly coloured with milk. Mr Jones introduced me as his son and nothing more was said.

Randle talked non-stop, wiping away at his worn face, pausing to sup from the bottle, turning to us when he wanted to emphasise something. In the fifteen minutes that followed how I fretted and longed to write everything down. The comedian was fluent, ranting on about show business, about that morning's walk-outs, about theatres and their quirks, about over-priced acts and tangles with the police, about cheating managers, about a ludicrous fight with a banjoist during which he, Randle (if he were to be believed), had broken the instrument over the player's head; about the rich culture of musical hall life.

I thrilled. It was pure poetry, a book dying to be written, a vanishing world of famous names, of singers and comedians, Gracie Fields, George Formby, Will Hay, Tommy Trinder and many others. He seemed to have met them all and I struggled woefully trying to remember essentials, my notebook stuck out of sight in a pocket.

Another worry was developing. It was becoming urgent to get back to the office and write up the night's review in time for tomorrow's paper.

Randle seemed set to go on even longer but we were cruelly interrupted. A glass fanlight stood open above the door and a loud voice sounded outside: "Where's that young reporter? Is he in there with Randle?"

It took a moment to sink in. The comedian swivelled on his chair. By now he was bleary eyed but still sharp-minded. "Are you a bloody reporter?" he demanded.

"It's a joke, it's a joke!" blustered the Hippodrome manager hastily pushing me to the door.

"I'll tan your bloody hide!" bellowed Randle staggering up.

But I was safely out in the passage where I came face to face with a national daily reporter, the man who had just blown my cover. He tried to get in and was arguing at the door as I pulled out my notebook, leant against a wall and frantically scribbled bits down before I forgot them. Randle slammed the door in the man's face and refused to see him, or anyone else.

The reporter was in his forties. He confronted me. "Did he say why the show walked out? What was the row about? What did he tell you?"

I shook my head. He wasn't going to get my precious notes.

The man eyed my notebook and I pushed it down into a pocket.

"Look! Give me the essentials. No one will know! I'll pay you."

He began to open his wallet but seeing the man's money somehow was counter-productive. It was just not me and I raced all the way back to the office, composing lines as I ran.

Mr Watson was at my side. He didn't hesitate. "Three paragraphs. No more. Just cover the show. We'll give the full story on Saturday. Now hurry!"

Others reporters concocted various versions of the story in the nationals in the days that followed, but the *Observer* was the lucky paper with the first-hand details. It was a good feeling.

But that wasn't all. Rowland came in from Redman's with another Randle incident. A man in Wednesday night's audience had shouted a string of obscenities and had thrown a tomato at the comedian. Randle had kept his composure, then startled everyone by throwing something back.

Rowland's face lit with a smile. Randle had thrown his false teeth.

Mr Jones, who was now keeping the *Observer* and, as it happened, the national dailies, well informed, said that a cleaner found the comedian's teeth under the stall seats. No one knew if the teeth had hit the man. One of the nationals, the *Daily Herald,* claimed they had - *Randle Snaps Back.*

On a lone visit to watch a play being rehearsed I explored the Hippodrome for myself. In its prime it was surely impressive, but everything seemed faded, a cavern of empty seats, and back-stage everything a bit tatty, in need of a coat of paint. Out if curiosity I climbed up into the Gods. The seats were so steep I sat down hurriedly. The stage seemed such a long way below. It felt like one could easily fall off and go crashing down.

Overall, despite attempts to keep going, music halls were declining. And there was a feeling that Accrington and East Lancashire itself were changing; even an outsider could sense it.

Several Methodist churches were experiencing smaller congregations. One became a furniture store, another turned into a garage annexe. Mills, too, seemed to be threatened. At times a tall unsmoking chimney caught the eye, contrasting noticeably with any that still belched their money-earning blackness.

There was still money in the town. Howard and Bullough's giant machinery works was reported to be turning out complete mills and selling them to organisations in the Far East. Would they become a threat and eventually undercut them? Folk said as much. But there were other troubles from time to time, redundancies, short-time working, and talk of strikes. A way of life - social, industrial, and economic – something that had started a couple of centuries earlier with the Industrial Revolution, it was changing. Rowland said he found it depressing and one day he intended to write a book about it.

18. Music Nights

On a cold afternoon Allan and Edith set off to visit their friends, the Birtwistles. We took a bus to Huncoat on the outskirts of Accrington and got out near the village stocks (ironically imprisoned in iron railings).

A twisting lane led down a hill to Childer's Green at Hapton. It was an old whitewashed farm building at the lane edge, single storey, with walls a couple of feet thick, a farm-holding with a useful field or two. Across the lane lay another farm and nearby was a small shiny lake or lodge, dammed at one end, and beyond it a view out over the Pennines.

Edith introduced me to Madge and Fred and to their son, Harry. The Birtwistles had run a small successful general bakery and confectioner's shop on the corner of Hood Street and Maudsley Street back in the town. There were plenty of customers. The Ewbank carpet sweeper factory was at the rear of their bakery and a foundry lay to one side. Workers from both places queued most weekdays for Birtwistles' pies and bread and cakes. Fred and Madge had a pet parrot and Fred made a point of putting its cage outside the shop on warm sunny days for all to see.

The shop was popular and did well. But Fred and Madge decided to change their style of life. They gave up the bakery and set up on a small-holding at Childer's Green at the edge of town. They became poultry farmers and kept hundreds of hens, as well as a few pigs.

Sitting at the fireside at Childer's we all had tea and talked the world to rights. Spring was coming and it was the first of several happy visits.

Harry and I were about the same age. He was intent on becoming a composer. His mother had bought him a clarinet when he was seven, and three or four years later he had written his first composition. He told me that sometimes he played the clarinet and saxophone in the orchestra pit at the Hippodrome Theatre. At school, too, he gave clarinet recitals when his school, St John's, had a concert. We got along all right and hiked around a bit. We went up onto Hameldon Hill, which rose beyond Accrington, and for me it was a memorable moment. For the first time I recognised a snipe, a long-billed bird my grandfather used to talk about and which he regarded as a symbol of good luck.

Later, Harry and I went on a week's fishing holiday at Ullswater in the Lake District, found a B and B in Patterdale village and climbed along Striding Edge ridge to the top of Helvellyn; we hired a rowboat intent on emptying Ullswater of fish. We didn't catch a thing, though we managed to get the rowboat under a strand of barbed wire, got past a *Private Keep Out* notice, and dragged the boat up a rocky river bed without being caught.

A day came when Harry, now 18, won a scholarship as clarinettist to the Royal Manchester College of Music and met fellow composers Alexander Goehr and Peter Maxwell Davies, the trumpeter Elgar Howarth and the pianist John Ogdon. With fellow students he founded the New Music Manchester group. Despite being away now in Manchester a lot of the time, he still visited the Lamberts occasionally, usually on Sunday evenings.

Edith pushed open the door of the front parlour at their Sandy Lane home and carried in plates loaded with scones and cakes. She was a generous calm woman. She had worked in a noisy cotton-weaving mill as a young woman, and like most of the men and women who worked there she was a skilled lip reader. Behind her quiet smile lay a bright perceptive intelligence. I came to love her dearly and was constantly amazed by her knowledge of music. Chopin was her favourite. Let a pianist get a few notes out of place during a radio performance then Edith noticed what had happened. If she mentioned it at all it was always quietly and with a wry smile. "That seemed to go a bit adrift, didn't it?"

But now: "Allan, leave the piano a moment will you? Help me pass the plates around."

Sunday night by the fireside. Six or so people filled the small front parlour, along with the grand piano, several low-down Edwardian chairs, a music stand overflowing with sheet music, and cups and saucers everywhere. The world nowadays seemed to be full of cups of tea. Several conversations were taking place at once and there were frequent bursts of laughter.

Besides Harry, who had brought his clarinet, another musician had come along, the pianist John Ogdon. He quickly admired Allan's beautiful Bechstein.

The room filled with music. Harry played his clarinet, Allan the piano, and then John was urged to play. Shyly he squatted on the piano stool. "I really don't know what to do," he confessed.

No one believed this. John was like a big friendly owl blinking slowly and Allan suggested a piece by Liszt. John's attention concentrated on the keys. The room about him, the cigarette smoke, friends and family seemingly ceased to exist. Portly and modest, his fingers rippled across the keyboard. In marvellous cascades the music rolled and thundered. Other pieces followed, and then: "What about your songs, Allan?"

Thanks to Harry, it seemed that John knew about Allan's *Old Pendle* songs. Pendle Hill lay to the north of Accrington and some years earlier Allan and a brother, Milton, had written a simple folksy song in its praise. They self-published it along with other modest songs.

Allan found the music and John began to play, first as Allan had written it, and then improvising round the theme, developing it and suddenly producing a version Chopin might have written. In the next few minutes miracles were wrought with Allan's simple song as John switched from one style to another – from Beethoven to Mendelssohn, from Scriabin to Mozart, and others. Allan was pink with admiration.

It was late before we broke up and people went their way home. It was a night we would remember.

Other Sunday night musical gatherings followed in the modest little parlour. For me, too, there were outings to Manchester where I met Sheila, Harry's fiancee. We ate large dishes of spaghetti and I slept on the floor at Sandy Goehr's flat, one he shared with Harry and others. On another visit to Childer's Sandy stayed there for Christmas and we walked up the lane to Huncoat and he talked about his father, Walter, the conductor and composer. One just never knew who next would be at Childer's.

If Allan's recurring favourite was Liszt's *Mephisto Valse,* which he played and played (humming at times in a somewhat distracting low drone), Edith did not always share his enthusiasm.

"Allan's not on with that again," she would say with a resigned though gentle groan.

Mischievously she even hid a bound copy of the *Mephisto* in a cupboard under a pile of newspapers. She gave a conspiratorial grin and whispered: "He'll get another copy," and of course he did, and had. Anticipating Edith's past behaviour, Allan had a reserve copy in a suitcase in their bedroom, though I had been sworn not to say so.

At times Edith would mention, hopefully though knowing it would never happen, that their little parlour would be more comfortable and there would be more room for visiting folk if Allan had a smaller piano. Allan of course would not hear of it, not that is, until he learned that he had been left a modest legacy amounting to a few thousand pounds. And a brilliant idea struck him.

In the days that followed, a new man walked down into Accrington's smoky town centre, chequebook at the ready. He gave the matter of his Bechstein some thought and went shopping. When Edith came in one afternoon the grand piano had been sold and had already been removed from the house; instead there were now two upright pianos. They stood against two of the parlour walls, one of course a superb Bechstein upright.

That done, Allan went back into town and bought a mass of duet music, a new piano stool and numerous other items, including a new grey scarf.

Unexpectedly the bank manager called. He had visited the Lamberts socially several times before, and had heard Allan play, indeed he played the violin himself though was always quick to confess he was not a very accomplished player. This time it was to mention that in the past five days Allan had overdrawn his legacy by several hundred pounds. I don't know how it was sorted out but Edith persuaded Allan to give her the chequebook and she presented it to the bank manager. Allan's legacy days were over.

The music of course wasn't. Allan's dear friend Ernest now sat at one of the pianos and Allan at the other and they worked happily through seemingly endless duets, including a series of second piano parts composed by Allan to all of Chopin's Etudes.

19. 7,000 Take a Trip

May was coming and the town's biggest employer, Howard and Bullough, known locally as Bullough's, was a hundred years old and the directors were intent on celebrating in style.

The giant textile machinery manufacturer – known as the Globe Works and at its zenith said to cover an astonishing 52 acres of floor space – decided to give its workers and their families a treat and take them to Blackpool for a day out. Amazingly, all 7,000 of them.

Mr Watson waved a schedule which had landed on his desk. "It's a good story. They're hiring special trains, and they're going to feed everyone!"

He turned to me and said that as I happened to come from Blackpool...which is how Garth and I got a day out and went to cover the outing.

Came the big day people swamped Accrington railway station. It was a precision day. At 7.38am, exactly on time, the first special express steamed in across the viaduct and halted at platform five where a long excited queue began to climb into the train's eleven carriages. It was scheduled to leave at 8.03. Supervised by the stationmaster, standing noticeably in a long dark coat with a watch in his hand, it did exactly that. In a rush of smoke and steam it puffed out of the station at 8,03 with the first 600 passengers.

The queue outside the station grew. It swelled and swelled until it was five people deep, and a hundred yards long. There was a lot of talk, and excitement increased as train after train arrived at the departure platform, loaded up and in a gush of smoke and steam, panted away, each shining engine (specially cleaned for the big day) bearing a centenary Bullough's plaque on the front of the boiler.

In Blackpool a barrage of press photographers and amazingly a hundred marshals were waiting at Central Station prepared to guide people about the resort. Garth was soon out of sight busy taking photographs.

Early showers gave way to sunny spells and the first arrivals escaped into the Tower and the Winter Gardens, using their free H & B centenary passes. The weather improved and Blackpool's golden sands, seven miles of them (Blackpool's publicity people especially asked for the figure to be mentioned) drew families down to the sea's edge and sand castle building took over.

Lunch for 7,000 needed two sittings. At eight of the nine restaurants which had been booked, a total of 3,500 people sat each time, and at teatime this happened all over again. Some 14,000 meals in all.

"Not many, if you say it quickly," said a tired Bullough's marshal.

Accrington kept Blackpool busy all day long and there was warm praise for Bullough's management.

At day-end, on a train back to Accrington I sat with a family and met a bemused father. He confessed that in all his forty years he had never once been to Blackpool and he had never ever seen the sea! Now at last he had been to Blackpool and believe it or not, he *still* hadn't seen the sea.

Ironically, he had gone to the town's South Shore, where the tide can go a long way out. And of course it had. It made a light gossip item in the paper, *He Saw the Sea At Last,* but I guessed he was a bit of a kidder, if not short-sighted.

The write-up and photographs in the *Observer* filled most of a page. The headline was simple: *Howard and Bullough's trip to Blackpool.*

Hundreds of extra *Observers* were sold and later Bullough's management, pleased by the generous coverage, treated the editorial staff to dinner at the posh Dunkenhalgh Hotel out at Clayton le Moors.

20. Wakes Week

Almost overnight Accrington turned into a ghost town. Everything was strangely quiet, the streets deserted, and many if not all of the town centre shops had closed.

If the immediate centre was empty, the railway station wasn't. It was under siege. People were pouring onto the main platform. The summer Wakes Weeks holiday had started and a mass of workers and their families were off to Blackpool.

Long trailing queues formed and there was a rush to board the Wakes Specials as they came steaming in across the viaduct. A little like the Bullough's centenary, though excitingly chaotic and not at all organised.

Rowland declared that when he was a boy his mother took him to Blackpool at Wakes Week: "It's an unpaid holiday. The factories and mills use it to do maintenance work. It used to be a week long, but it seems to becoming two.

"All our street packed up and went off to Blackpool, just like that! Mother made me wear my name and address on a label tied in a buttonhole, in case I got lost on the sands. Of course I was only little, and lots of others were the same. Some years we couldn't afford to go and we bought in lots of food for the week because shops weren't open. Instead, if we were lucky, we'd go on a bus on day trips."

Towns around Accrington held their Wakes holidays at different times. Blackpool simply could not hold all Lancashire at once.

"Of course posh people go to Southport or even Morecambe," said Rowland. "But mother knew Blackpool was best."

There were trips to other places, including the Lake District and Wales. Mystery outings were advertised in which people booked tickets, not knowing their destination.

Wakes Weeks was one thing if you were happily enjoying the seaside but back in town little was happening. With everyone seemingly away ("Even the burglars," quipped Frank) the next edition of the *Observer* was going to be thin on news. We were struggling for stories.

Then Allan said he had heard about a man who had built a yacht all by himself, or built something, but probably he would be away in Blackpool. He thought the man lived up Ormerod Street, but it probably wasn't true. Mr Watson sent me to find out.

It turned out to be a good little story. The man was a joiner and not only had he built a 12ft wooden sailing dinghy, but the surprise was that he had built it in the front room of his terrace house.

It was a beautiful craft, clinker built, shiny with varnish. It took up just about the whole of the room where it rested on two stands, the bows facing the bay window.

"Six thousand screws," the owner informed me, as I pondered the obvious question: how was he going to it out of the room? It certainly would not go through the door.

"All facing fore and aft," he added proudly. "The slots."

Every screw was aligned with the window. And of course that was how he got the dinghy into the street... he removed the window one weekend and it went out through the bay, which became the headline.

21. Helping Stanley

The weeks and months sped by. Another December loomed. Another junior reporter called Mickey had joined the staff. He had a thin face and seemed a bit smart, but he was pleasant enough.

Allan and Mr Harry started muttering together, pouring over a manuscript spread on Mr Harry's desk, writing in a word or two, discussing the changes, crossing things out. It happened in odd quiet moments. Back at home Allan kept disappearing into the front room and tinkling on the Bechstein. Edith grumbled that he was always late for meals.

"Reporters!" she said. "*I-my-me. Three-times-plural!*"

But at last it was explained. Allan and Harry Crossley had written a song for Accrington Stanley.

The soccer club had been experiencing numerous ups and downs, yet even outsiders had heard of the town's team. Mention

Accrington to a stranger and immediately they would respond: *"Accrington Stanley!"*

The town was proud of its soccer club. Even the soccer pitch was distinctive for it had a kind of rise in the middle. As a result if a match was going wrong, the crowd shouted: "Keep it on the island!" Likewise, similar cries when the ball went over the top into the road outside.

The club enjoyed considerable good will and many wanted it to survive, especially Mr Watson, who was a dedicated supporter. Accrington without the Reds would seem unthinkable. Yet there was unease. There were times when the Reds seemed to be losing too many matches.

The unease seemed to exist in the town, too, The *Observer* was doing well, both in circulation and advertising revenue, but the town – once the undisputed centre of the cotton and textile machinery industries - seemed to be faltering and there was more talk of redundancies and strikes. Even the threat to the Hippodrome seemed part of it.

It didn't seem much, but on Saturday mornings a group of us went to the club's Peel Park ground to clear up any rubbish and rake the ash level round the pitch. Every little helped and now, in their own way, Allan and Mr Harry were having a go of their own.

Their song, *On Stanley On,* was published by the *Observer* and it caught on with the club's supporters.

The day came when the Reds competed in the third round of the FA Cup for the first time since the 1936-1937 season. The Accrington Male Voice Choir spent a lot of time recorded the song and to encourage the team it was played over loudspeakers at Peel Park during the FA Cup match against Tranmere Rovers. The game ended in a 2-2 draw.

Four days later, disappointingly, at Tranmere, the Reds lost the replay, 5-1. Despite this the song grew in popularity and Stanley's supporters sang it frequently.

On Stanley On

by Harry Crossley and Allan Lambert

Stanley's a team that we all talk about;
Their name and fame are spreading far and wide;
They're on the map, it's true.
They're sportsmen through and through
Are the gallant lads in red who've turned the tide.
Chorus
On Stanley, on lads - on Stanley, on!
We'll cheer our heads off
When you get that ball in the net; and so it's

On Stanley, on lads; we'll fight until we've won.
Be sure we'll never be downhearted.
Cos it's on Stanley on!

People genuinely liked the song and Allan and Mr Harry were pleased. They gave a specially signed copy to Mr Watson who had the words framed.

22. Gentlemen of the Press

The office was awash with another Harold Taylor upset. Another reporter had left.

There was talk about Accrington sending a replacement. But though several of us debated which of us it would be, nothing happened until Saturday morning and another edition of the paper was out in the shops.

Mr Watson called me into his office. I waited for the bad news.

"You seem to be getting on all right," he told me. "I wonder if you'd like a change?"

I tried to look as if I didn't.

"I want you to cover Rishton for us," he said. "Fred's decided to leave and I need someone to replace him."

Rishton! It was about four miles from Accrington.

He observed my relief.

"I thought it was going to be Haslingden," I told him.

Mr Watson's face turned a shade severe. "No, Harold says he's going to choose the new reporter himself, so we're leaving it to him."

It meant I was about to become a district reporter in charge of news gathering in a small town. I knew nothing about Rishton but I couldn't have been happier.

"You'll like Rishton," said Frank.

Fred Billington said he would show me round before he left. I scarcely knew him. He was about thirty-five, lean and his nose was a little bent. He told me it had been broken when he had been a boxer.

On a bright morning we caught a bus from Accrington and ten minutes later at Clayton le Moors we changed into another bus to Rishton.

Fred said that Rishton had once had as many as ten cotton mills at different times down the years; and coal mining. But many Rishtonians now found work out of town in Blackburn and Accrington and elsewhere.

"You come once a week. Visit all the contacts and write up any stories for the Rishton page. Don't worry, I'll show you."

"Supposing there aren't any?"

"You keep looking till you find something."

He knocked at a door. "This is our new district reporter," he said, introducing me to a constable.

The man raised his eyebrows, but comically. "Oh yes? Well I hope you make a better job than Fred. But don't go expecting us to be all friendly when you come on the phone asking daft questions."

Next, the Roman Catholic priest, a tired looking man, rather careworn, though pleasant enough.

"Are you RC? You're not? I see we'll have to work on you."

After this we called on the clerk to the council who greeted us with an uneasy smile.

Fred had a copy of the monthly council minutes and with the clerk's help managed to fill out several small items to make them into passable stories.

"He's wary is that one," Fred commented as we left. "He'd prefer it if we didn't call on him."

At the manse the Methodist minister sat us in a long room with a one-bar electric fire glowing in the middle. It was cold and the fire was having a struggle. But there was news enough: a Rishton family emigrating to Canada, two deaths, and a presentation to a Sunday school teacher. All good Methodists.

Calls followed now on shops, the undertakers, and then to the cricket club to see if a decision had been made about repairs to a building. Last of all, a visit to the Vicar.

The vicarage door opened to reveal a white haired man.

"Good morning," began Fred.

The vicar stared at me. "And who the hell are you?"

This was not a greeting I had expected from a vicar. I raised my hand to shake his but he offered his left hand because the other one was injured. It was an awkward start. Yet in the coming weeks he always seemed glad to see me, and he did give me a story or two.

In the meantime I was on my own. A district reporter. I had sort of graduated. Sort of. Each week I took the buses to Rishton and gradually came to know the little town, combing it for news items, and I was lucky for somehow there was always something worth reporting, often parochial, sometimes a bit lacking in detail, the nitty-gritty, but even so usually readable for Rishton folk. It was a challenge and gradually I began to extend the Rishton coverage.

There were poignant moments. I knocked at a cottage door. "Good morning, is this where Mr Walton lived? I'm from the *Observer*."

The small crinkle-faced woman opened the door a bit wider, her black felt hat a little askew. She turned round and called. "S'all right, Mary, it's t'lad from *t'Observer*." She smiled faintly. "Come in, lad. I've been expecting you."

A single step off the pavement onto the carpeted floor of a darkened front room.

Obituaries were the worst of jobs. Gentleness, and the need to listen quietly. The man's name, Albert Walton, his age, fifty-two; his work, twenty years as a miner, eighteen as...

"Yes," said Mrs Walton solemnly. "That's right. He dug graves. Albert said he never could stop digging so when he gave up at t'pit he got with the corporation over at t'cemetery."

Suddenly remembering: "But do you want to see him, love?"

She turned to a white-shrouded object, which I noticed for the first time. She pulled back the cover and revealed the rigid body of Albert Walton lying flat out on a table next to a wall.

"Eh," said Mrs Walton gently, a world of compassion in her old voice, and softly she said: "But he were a lovely man."

I can hear her now.

My shorthand was improving, but not fast enough and it let me down. A meeting of Rishton Urban District Council arrived. The chairman, decked in a chain of office, rose to his feet, coughed, looked at his notes and began to speak to the councillors sitting round the council table. He was sorry to be giving up like this, but he knew everyone would understand that there were now other commitments, matters he could not avoid as well as other matters. Going and coming. In all his time as chairman, a grand time, and also a sad one as many well knew with illness, not one anyone could look back on without feeling that the town was making progress...

Well, as he had pointed out, he was sorry to be giving up, but he wished to thank everyone for being so helpful, especially ...nay, particularly the Gentlemen of the Press, and of course their hard working clerk who kept them all in good order, and he was sorry it was happening because...

He went on and the two Gentlemen of the Press, the evening reporter from Blackburn and me, took it down in shorthand and at the same time tried to work it all out.

The evening reporter said as we left: "Well that was a right bugger's muddle!"

Back at the office next morning I struggled to turn it into a short report. Even the slow-speaking chairman had been too quick for my shorthand and there were woeful gaps, but I wrote it up and it appeared in the Saturday *Observer.*

The phone rang in Reporters and a grim faced Mr Harry handed me the receiver.

"What's this nonsense about me leaving the council?" demanded an angry voice. It was the Rishton chairman. "You've made me a laughing stock. I'm on the council another year yet. What? No, of course I'm not giving up. I've resigned as council chairman. Yes, I want a full apology..."

My misery was acute. Having dismissed the chairman from the council in one edition, I had to reinstate him as a councillor, once in the Tuesday edition, and again the following Saturday.

I told Mr Watson: "I really believed he was leaving the council. The evening paper man thought so too."

But that was no excuse. The difference was, the evening paper reporter had telephoned the council clerk later to check the facts. I should have done the same.

Mr Harry was annoyed. "No one is born accurate. Accuracy has to be learned. Let me see your shorthand notes."

We found my scrawled Rishton pages.

"You need to improve your shorthand. Just make sure you get it right next time. And if you are unsure, check it again."

With Vic, I retreated into our favourite café and over a cup of tea he commiserated. "Cheer up. You're not the first to get something wrong. I had a bad do a year back."

Mr Watson had informed him that there was a woman at the front office counter wanting to see the reporter who had written that she was dead. Appalled, Vic had gone downstairs to see her.

"Are you the gormless reporter who says I'm dead?" the woman had demanded. "Well, I'm *not!*"

Vic, who told us he had been stumped – his word - and at a loss to know what to say, had blurted out: "Well, you're *glad* aren't you?"

This unexpected response somehow had robbed the woman of her next criticism and she had laughed and gone away.

"So you see," said Vic, "you're not the only one to get something wrong. As it was, there were two sisters. I'd polished off the wrong one."

Vic was trying to cheer me up, and he did. But the fact remained, I had not been careful enough and it did not feel good. No paper likes to be let down and have to print an apology.

"Once a mistake is in print it's there for ever," said Mr Watson.

Later by chance I met the sacked chairman in the street and told him I was sorry for the misunderstanding. He said he had got over it and worse things had happened in the war.

Council meetings did not always produce stories. Rishton again, and the *Telegraph* reporter from Blackburn was there. The meeting was brief and almost immediately the councillors went into private session, a practice that annoyed reporters, if no one else. Perhaps thirty or forty minutes travel to get to the meeting and the whole thing over in moments.

"To hell with this," said the evening reporter as we left without a single item of news.

"I've timed the meeting," he said. "What's more I timed the last one. It was four minutes and twenty seconds that time, and tonight it was only three minutes and twenty five seconds. Are you game we both put in a par saying the council has beaten its own record for public business by ninety-five seconds? We'll show them!"

It suited me. The so-called public meetings were often a farce. Few wanted to say anything out in the open.

The single-paragraph story appeared in both papers and the *Observer* version resulted in an indignant letter of protest from Rishton, though noticeably at the next council meeting several items were discussed in public, which made the news pages.

The Vicar and I got to know one another. We talked about our favourite books and how he had always wanted to be a musician, to play the cello, but his injured hand had made it impossible. He said that Rishton years earlier had been tremendously busy. At one time there had been some eight thousand looms running in the town's mills, but one by one the works had been closing.

"It looks like another's going to go, the Albert mill. There's a lot of talk in the town."

On another visit he gave me a story about a couple of runaways, a young Rishton girl and a boy from the next town, Great Harwood. Gone to Scotland, he thought.

Gretna?

Perhaps. But would I keep his name out of it?

Apparently the girl's father had gone to Great Harwood to her boyfriend's home and had hammered on the door prepared to give him a beating. But the boy's mother had pushed the lad into a cupboard where he stayed hidden until the man had gone. The next thing was the two youngsters had run away.

I went to the girl's home in Rishton and met her mother. She told me that she had urged them to run away and get married. She told me this in front of her husband as I strove to write it down, glaring at him to stop him interrupting. But the man broke in and said he would knock out the lad's brains once he got hold of him.

"You shut your trap," the woman snapped. "You'll leave 'em alone or I'll call the police."

She sounded pretty tough, with arms and hands noticeably as big as her husband's. Apparently the two had a coal delivery cart.

At the door, as I left, she added for my benefit that she knew where they were going to live, not in Rishton anyway, and she had bought them a nice wedding present, two thick army blankets for their bed. And she thought he was a nice boy and they would be all right.

Mr Watson read the story. "Are you sure about this?"

"Absolutely. It was the girl's mother who told me, and her husband heard it all. I've checked it over with her."

The story, suitably edited, was nosed on the fact that it was the boy's mother who had hidden him in a cupboard to escape a beating, and the girl's mother who had urged the couple to run away. It made the Saturday Rishton page. Saved by two mums.

For a time I hoped to meet up with the runaways and hear their side, but they seemed to have moved to Preston, well clear of the girl's father.

I was enjoying Rishton. Mr Watson decided to add on Oswaldtwistle.

23. Splash Story

Oswaldtwistle seemed to be one long road, Union Road. The often-blackened buildings and cobbled streets felt old. The town looked old. It *was* old. Of course many streets branched off with faded lines of what I guessed were weavers' or miners' cottages, solid stone and brick, but Union Road seemed to dominate them all. Lots of pubs, many of them closed down, their etched glass panels in doors still bearing their names. Rowland told me how many but I forgot the number. I think he said that once there were fifty.

Everyone seemed to call the town Ossy, with the township of Church, or Church Kirk, at the lower end.

Cotton textiles once dominated, with spinning and weaving mills, print and chemical works, coalmining and quarries. A hard working town. Its older industries no longer dominant.

Once more like Rishton. Weekly calls on shop keepers and pubs, and yet another town clerk who never had any stories, because nothing ever happened in Oswaldtwistle. He didn't say that exactly, but it was the impression he gave: a man who sat at a desk able to hold an entire conversation without ever once looking into your face.

Again there were calls on the religious leaders, the undertakers, the library, sometimes a school. And always there was something.

Garth picked me up from the office. We were due at a nursery opening. An Oswaldtwistle photograph, which was good. A picture always brightened the page.

"It'll save a wait at the bus stop if we go in my car," Garth explained.

In cheerful mood, we set off from Accrington half an hour before the opening ceremony. We took a short cut over a ridge and bumped and rattled along a series of cobbled streets. Once over the high bit the going was easier. In third gear, we began to run downhill, edged in by grey stone houses but today smog free, a clear sky and a view of the hills.

Garth said: "Did you feel something?"

The car had lurched.

Out of the window I saw a dark object bounding alongside. It bounced, keeping pace then, as we juddered abruptly to an emergency halt, our nearside back wheel ran on past us and rolled down a pavement into a wall. The car sank back on one side.

We abandoned the vehicle by the kerb, loaded ourselves with photographic gear, including a monstrous state-of-the-art flashgun and charger in a shiny brown varnished heavy wooden case, which Garth carried on one sagging shoulder. We trudged the rest of the way to the nursery on foot.

We were late but nothing had started. Oswaldtwistle Urban District Council chairman wearing his shiny civic chain was waiting, the Labour councillors in chalk stripe suits were waiting, the Conservatives, several in pin stripes, were waiting, the matron, nursery staff and a selection of scrubbed children and babies were waiting; without a photographer it was no good trying to hold an official opening because a mere write-up in the paper without a picture didn't seem as impressive.

Looking amazingly calm considering his car had just lost a wheel, Garth organised the nursery photo and the relief was noticeable.

Holding a baby encased in waterproofs, the council chairman dibbled a hand in a children's water trough.

"A little smile, Mr Chairman, if you please," urged Garth. The chairman and councillors smiled. There was a click as the flash failed to flash.

"Sorry…"

Again the pose, again a dibble in the trough, a floating yellow duck picked up for the baby to see, again no flash.

Garth, a strained look developing, adjusted his camera and examined the new flashgun.

The nursery suddenly seemed to be full of tense-looking people. The children fidgeted, there was splashing, the chairman's hand was pink if not blue, the matron, middle aged and anxious about any upset to her schedule, looked several times as if she were about to intervene but each time decided against it. At last the flash went off and the baby looked surprised and then screamed.

For once, reporter and photographer refused the offer of tea and sandwiches. We hurried away to catch a bus back to the office, conscious that the chairman's trousers had suffered badly and looked as if he had wet himself.

"All the splashing," said Garth. "Good of him not to complain."

"It was the matron's face that frightened me."

The photograph came out perfectly. Carefully touched up, it made a handsome picture in Saturday's *Observer*. The mothers would buy copies. Every face… especially babies'.

Most of the trekking round Oswaldtwistle happened during the day, but from time to time there were evening events, including a Working Men's Club presentation of a musical operetta, *The Desert Song*.

The stage filled with singing men in flowing crimson and lemon robes, their faces covered in cocoa. They were in good voice, cheerful and boisterous, stocky, working men, singing well, their polished boots occasionally showing beneath their Arabian robes.

To the delight of the audience there was also a live horse.

"Ah!" cried the leading singer dramatically. "*Eere* comes Red Shadow." At once, ten left arms swung out and pointed to the side of the stage, but somehow it didn't happen as everyone expected because the horse and Red Shadow came on from the other side. A moment's confusion and startled stares all round, then ten right arms swung up in one combined swing and pointed across to the other side as if the whole thing had been planned.

A couple of popular songs were sung and the horse, amazingly placid, stood under the spotlights, staring unmoving into the theatre.

The audience was full of admiring whispers and only slowly did people become aware of an uncomfortable smell.

Red Shadow, sitting upright in his flaring crimson cloak, noticed it too and began to edge his steed towards the wings, making his exit, the horse leaving a calling card for one of the cast to scoop up with a shovel and brush, a detail not mentioned in the *Observer's* revue.

It was a happy, cheerful night out.

24. Gym-slip Caller

One morning I learned that Geraldine had left and a girl called Audrey Gray was occupying her desk.

Audrey was sixteen and caused an instant stir. She was decidedly attractive and had taken over writing *Ladies' Chain*. She had a confident manner and a quick bright smile.

It came out that a year earlier she had inquired about a possible job at the *Observer*. At that time, still only fifteen, she was on her way to school in her native Blackburn when someone mentioned that the newspaper was looking for a junior girl reporter.

She abandoned all thought of going to school that day and acted at once. As she said: "I thought: 'Blow school!'"

Impulsively she got on a bus to Accrington, reached the *Observer* office, and still wearing a gym-slip and clutching her satchel, asked if she could see the editor.

Her timing was lucky. Mr Watson saw her. But it seemed to go nowhere. "Well, we haven't really got a job," he told her.

Audrey said: "But he spoke kindly and I just hoped. He was such a lovely man."

A year later the paper did advertise for a junior reporter and she tried again. She got an interview and Mr Watson, remembering the initiative of the gym-slip girl, gave her the job, adding appreciatively: "And you've not come with your parents."

Job-seekers, it seems, usually arrived with support, making editors groan.

Everybody was keen about Audrey. Mr Harry definitely was. "She can certainly write," he enthused. Then, perhaps because he had sounded too enthusiastic: "But she can't spell!" He was quite eager. So were the men in the caseroom where a variety of remarks went the rounds.

Audrey was being paid 30 shillings a week. It seemed very little and made my £3 weekly seem a fortune. Writing *Ladies' Chain* column took some doing and only occasionally did she show any signs of tension though she confessed that she wept a bit now and then, in the privacy of the Ladies.

She was now part of the tea-making brigade. She encountered the roller towel in the tiny washroom. Drying the cups and mugs after washing up meant trying to find a bit of the towel that was deep grey, rather than black. A cub reporter's perk.

Soon she was writing more than the woman's column. She went out on general reporting jobs, including up to Haslingden where, apparently, even Harold got on with her. Not that he would have had much choice; Audrey seemed capable of dealing with an awkward man.

Garth set out with Audrey in his car to do a Haslingden story. In the middle of nowhere the car broke down. He had run out of petrol. Audrey had to wait while he walked to the nearest garage to buy more. Back in Accrington, Garth got plenty of stick. The printers, as usual, managed to make a meal out of the whole thing.

Audrey had a stormy side as we learned. She was called in to Mr Richard's office.

He was reading her expenses claim which totalled one shilling and twopence for the week.

"What's this?" he demanded, examining the figures. "Couldn't you walk rather than get a bus?"

Audrey was outraged. She could hardly believe that he was quibbling over such a small sum.

Angrily she blurted out: "You are a MEAN old man!"

She left the room quickly, suddenly aware that her job at the *Observer* was in danger of ending.

It was not long before Mr Watson appeared in Reporters. He was looking grim and called her into his office.

Everyone soon knew all the details.

"Mr Richard is furious," he had told her. "But I don't want to lose you."

"One and tuppence!" she told him.

A difficult time followed for Mr Watson. He begged and pleaded with Mr Richard not to insist that Audrey should be sacked. Mr Harry joined him and backed him up. It took a lot of diplomatic effort.

In the end, she kept her job, but only just. The two men saved her.

"It wasn't like me," confessed Audrey. "But just imagine it, *one and tuppence!*"

And that was that. She was lucky. She kept her job and heard nothing more.

25. Stories That Didn't Make It

Sometimes good news stories were there but did not make the *Observer's* pages. An Oswaldtwistle newsagent tipped me off that the council was caught up in a boundary dispute. A row was going on about a house: no one could decide whether the house was in Oswaldtwistle or in Accrington.

So a visit to see Oswaldtwistle's council clerk: I had discovered, though it was no surprise, that he had been a solicitor. Professionally tight lipped. Of course he said that he knew nothing about any boundary dispute. Back then to the newsagent who insisted that something funny was definitely going on.

A half-pint in a pub produced more information, all unconfirmed. The landlord said the councillors were arguing about which council was entitled to the rates from the house. It seemed the boundary ran through the middle of the house.

It sounded a flimsy tale. The landlord said: "They say the boundary goes right through the old man's bed! So that's a queer 'un."

It definitely sounded flimsy, but still a good story if true.

But where was the house?

I asked around in shops, and a string of contacts, but no one seemed to know. The story was never written, though the newsagent, whenever we met, always asked if anything had materialised. It may be that in the end it had not happened. There was never a mention in the council minutes.

More dramatic, another story that never got into the paper, though it had everyone talking, happened at Haslingden a year or two before my time.

Some old property in the town was demolished higher up from the lych gate at St James Church. The buildings backed up to the churchyard and apparently the contractor had failed to secure the retaining wall before starting demolition. The wall collapsed and coffins and skeletons tumbled out of the graveyard and landed down in the main road.

Everyone in the *Observer* office had known it had happened; everyone in Haslingden likewise must have known, but as far as anyone could tell the story never appeared in the paper.

Had it been censored? Had it been held out deliberately? Was the vicar involved? Was a worried well-known Haslingden family involved? Did it ever appear in print elsewhere, if not in the *Observer?*

It was before Tom Watson's time, but people still mentioned it.

Rowland came into Reporters and sank down at his desk looking exhausted.

Mr Harry put down the phone: "Rowland, whatever's the matter?"

Something was. Rowland's face was the colour of ash and his raincoat had a long gash down one side.

"It was a bull! I've just been chased by a bull."

And he had, only yards from the office.

Rowland had been crossing over as two men drove the bull down Edgar Street, apparently on the way to the abattoirs in Hyndburn Road.

Rowland was still shaking. He took off his ruined coat and we made him a cup of tea with three sugars.

He told us the bull had put its head down and had charged.

"I got into a doorway and it seemed to come straight at me! But I got the door open and got inside. There was a terrible crash as it hit the wall!"

In fact the door had fallen open behind him and Rowland had tumbled inside, tearing the coat.

We had all seen cows being driven past the front of the office from time to time on their way to the abattoirs, but this was the first time one of us had seen a bull.

"I wouldn't care," said Rowland, "but mother's only just bought me this raincoat."

"It's a good story," said Frank. "I'll write it up. It'll make Saturday's second splash! *Journalist escapes charging bull death!*"

But we all knew that Mr Watson would not print it. It was one of his rules.

"Our job is to report the news, not make it."

Rowland didn't want it in, either.

Frank said that Rowland at least ought to charge the *Observer* for a new raincoat. "After all, it was in your work hours."

But Rowland didn't. His mother sewed it up and at Christmas she bought him a new one.

26. Locked Door

Mr Harry had sent me round to Garth's studio with a packet of negatives and I walked back through the town-centre past a terrace of small stone houses. They were being demolished and two had already been reduced to rubble but a third was still standing. Was something the matter? The demolition men seemed to be arguing.

A man from the housing department, who did not want his name mentioned, discretely showed me the demolition order. Three houses had to come down, but they had just realised that the third building in the row in fact was two small homes, though at a first glance it looked as if it were only one. No one knew who owned this fourth dwelling, which was unoccupied. The door was locked and the housing man didn't know what to do. He retreated for a long time into a phone box. Whatever the rights or wrongs of the matter, he came back and said the fourth building would have to be demolished as well and they had to go ahead. Using a sledgehammer, a workman broke open the door and we all went in.

We stepped into the past. The living kitchen and its flagged floor was thick in cobwebs and dust. Scarcely any light reached inside for the single window facing the street was black with years of grime. All that remained of the curtain that had once hung across it were a few shrivelled yellow shreds dangling from a wire. The house was creepy.

Whoever had lived there evidently had been expecting to return because crumpled paper and sticks, heavily coated in soot, had been set in the cast iron grate ready for lighting. A pegged mat lay before it and started to come apart as we trod on it.

The person seemed to have been a hoarder. A small side space off the living room was full of empty bottles and jars, all stacked neatly on stone shelves. There was a slop stone and a battered dolly tub, and a mangle with wooden rollers, both of the rollers bleached near-white and badly worn in the middle where clothes had once squeezed through.

A heap of old newspapers provided a clue. We were surprised. They were dated 1938. Had the house been empty all those years? It was beginning to look like it.

Both upstairs and down, the place was amazingly dry. The most telling object in the house was a dust-covered rock-like lump on the kitchen table. It was all that remained of a packet of sugar. Had it been on the table during the whole of the 1939-45 War? It seemed so and the workmen could only marvel that mice or rats had not eaten it to bits.

The gloomy old cottage made a short article in the paper, and a week or two later it resulted in a second story. Mr Watson received a letter from an Accrington man, who was living now in Surrey, and we learned that his aunt had been living in the house by herself all those years ago and had become ill. She had been taken to hospital where she had died. The door of the little stone house had been locked ever since.

The range of stories landing on my desk started to change. Mr Watson said: "You're coming on. Your shorthand's a lot better and I'm going to switch you to more general news."

A headmaster retiring, a toolroom strike at Bullough's, another inquest, a long service in memory of the Pals, seventy redundancies at an Oswaldtwistle mill, a car crash outside Veever's grocery shop – they were a welcome change. I would miss Rishton but there was plenty to write about in Accrington.

Rowland of course knew about the Pals. A First World War massacre. A battalion of 1,100 Pals – the 11th East Lancashire Regiment, all of them volunteers – had included some 250 men from Accrington. In July 1916 on their first day of action at Sierre in northern France, half the battalion was wiped out. Within half an hour 235 were killed or missing and 350 wounded. A bitter memory.

Rishton, meanwhile, became the responsibility of Audrey. She soon encountered a corpse or two. Calling at a dead person's house to do a modest write-up resulted sometimes in a courteous invitation to step inside. I'd found out that much for myself.

But Audrey beat us all. She arrived back at her desk, a bit flushed. She had seen three corpses in one morning.

"They seem to keep the body for two or three days. Well you can't say no, can you, when they ask if you would like to step inside and see their lost one? You can't hurt their feelings."

We exchanged notes and decided that the kind of contacts we disliked most was working men's clubs, especially early morning after the club had had a busy night before.

"I just hate that smell of stale beer and cigarette smoke!" Audrey said.

I agreed. They had a flavour all of their own.

Saturday, the paper out in the shops and streets, a day off. Another visit in the afternoon to Harry's for tea and, as it happened, unexpectedly a further story. There was trouble at nearby Huncoat. Coal mining was causing subsidence in the surrounding land and it was alleged it was causing the cracks in walls and ceilings in many of the farm buildings. There seemed no doubt about it. Harry's dad, Fred, was looking grim as he pointed to cracks in the ceiling at Childer's. The room had not long been decorated.

Walking back up the lane to Huncoat I wondered if other people were having similar trouble. A spur-of-the moment call at a worn looking house showed they were, and at once there was a story for the paper. The owner and his wife were still angry. They said they had been asleep in bed and had been frightened out of their wits when the ceiling had fallen in on them.

"Not the whole ceiling?"

"No, but too bloody much if it!"

The man was furious and was demanding that the National Coal Board paid them compensation.

The *Observer* printed the story and other people in the area began to complain that walls and ceilings in their homes were showing similar cracks. The story seemed to go on for weeks. It even got in the nationals and the

Daily Herald joined in again: *Coal Board Gets Cracking.*

I did a couple of feature articles and at Accrington central library an assistant, Kay Hindle, helped with the research. We became friends and went on several outings including a bus trip to Manchester where she met up with Harry at a concert. Kay left Accrington on a two-year librarian course at a college in Leeds, but I continued to take the Manchester bus. On the return late one night the double-decker came to a halt in heavy fog, visibility down to a couple of yards. Everyone stood around fearing another vehicle might come crashing into the back of us.

It was urgent we kept moving. We gathered up newspapers from inside the bus and three of us started to walk on in front through the fog, and the bus crawled along behind, its headlights shining on the papers. A four-mile-an-hour crawl. It just worked and eventually we walked out of the thickest patches of mist and got back to Accrington a couple of hours late.

It made a short item in the *Observer* and it was a surprise when a version also appeared in the *Daily Herald*. But it was not quite the same story. Some smart alec had improved the tale. In the *Herald* the passengers had walked in front lighting the way with cigarette lighters.

27. Vic to the Rescue

A fresh summer and with it came the cricket season. At once there were more matches each Saturday than the *Observer* had staff available to cover them. For the first time as a result I became part of the cricket reporting team, in my case a doubtful honour, doubtful that is from the *Observer's* point of view.

Playing cricket in the park in my teens had been one thing (better at bowling than batting); writing up cricket matches for the *Observer* was another. It became a weekly task and I failed miserably. Again and again I went to matches, wrote them up, and gave the reports to Vic to check, or, if he were away, to Guy Cunliffe in his little den. Usually they were accurate enough, though not exactly entertaining.

"Cricket writing is not my strength," I told Vic, and he agreed.

"You're no Neville Cardus, that's a fact! Perhaps you're better at music."

Nonetheless my cricket reports were printed, suitably edited. Usually I got the bowling parts right.

Audrey now did stints at copy-holding for Guy, though none of us knew if she enjoyed cricket. The caseroom men were always interested whenever she passed through to the proof-reader's little den.

Another Accrington fire story came my way. It was a slight affair compared with the blaze at Bridge's but I was feeling asthmatic and Vic noticed that I was struggling a bit.

The fire was in a terrace house in Bold Street and unusually we heard about it after it was over and the firemen had put it out.

Mr Harry sent me to try to locate the family and get an interview. I knocked at several doors and found they were staying further up the street with the husband's brother. Over a cup of tea they told me what had happened.

Back at the office, Vic said: "So what's up?"

I'd typed the start; and then typed it again. It should have been all right but it wasn't.

He came and squatted alongside.

"It's not coming right," I told him.

Vic read it for himself.

Fire gutted an Accrington house in Bold Street on Wednesday. The tenants Mr and Mrs J. Pearson were in the kitchen when a pan of fat burst into flames.

Despite the danger Mr Pearson dashed upstairs to rescue their baby from his cot.

Mr Pearson told an Observer reporter: "It happened that quick! There was lots of smoke and flames. Even in our Billy's bedroom! It's lucky we got out alive."

Vic pointed. "The start's in your second par. How old is the father?"

I didn't know.

"What about the baby?"

It was six months.

"Right. How about:

"An Accrington father rescued his six-month baby son from a blazing house on Wednesday."

That was much better.

"In fact," he added, "make it*: An heroic Accrington father..."*

I had a high regard for Vic and started again, using his opening par, chopping out words.

Frank of course had to get a look in. "How about: *Heroic dad saves screaming blaze baby?"*

He must have seen my expression. However, Mr Watson didn't like screaming blaze baby either. "We're not the *Mirror* yet," he said.

His own headline turned out to be longer but more in tune with the *Observer's* quiet tradition: *Father rescues baby son from blazing house.* It made a top-of-the page story in Saturday's paper. I read it in bed, where I stayed for a day or two until the asthma had passed.

28. Moving On

The years came and went. The *Observer* building, with its engaging tangle of lives, its maze of passages and small rooms, was demolished and for a time became a muddy car park. In Blackburn Road, a token *Observer* office opened for a while and then an outlet was established in the Market Hall.

The *Observer* itself, no longer full of adverts on the front page, was given a New Look, a smaller tabloid size, smart, modern, brilliant colour photographs, printed in Oldham, and owned by the Trinity Mirror Group.

Some of the people...

Allan and Edith retired to Lowick Green in the Lake District where Allan played on his beloved upright Bechstein. I landed in Fleet Street at *The Daily Telegraph* foreign desk, and Audrey Gray, under her married name, Eyton, founded the famous *F-Plan diet* and wrote a best-selling book.

And the musicians...

All renowned: John Ogdon, composer and pianist; Sandy, Alexander Goehr, composer and Professor of Music at Cambridge; Max, Sir Peter Maxwell Davies, composer and Master of the Queen's Music; and Harry, Sir Harrison Birtwistle, composer, controversial, a Lancashire lad, world famous.

If only the baker could know the whole tale.

www.ingramcontent.com/pod-product-compliance
Lightning Source LLC
Chambersburg PA
CBHW061949070426
42450CB00007BA/1106